Stack-n-Whackier
QUILTS

BETHANY S. REYNOLDS

American Quilter's Society
P. O. Box 3290 • Paducah, KY 42002-3290
www.AQSquilt.com

Located in Paducah, Kentucky, the American Quilter's Society (AQS) is dedicated to promoting the accomplishments of today's quilters. Through its publications and events, AQS strives to honor today's quiltmakers and their work and to inspire future creativity and innovation in quiltmaking.

EDITOR: BARBARA SMITH
ILLUSTRATIONS: WILLIAM W. REYNOLDS
GRAPHIC DESIGN: ELAINE WILSON
COVER DESIGN: MICHAEL BUCKINGHAM
QUILT PHOTOGRAPHY: CHARLES R. LYNCH
HOW-TO PHOTOGRAPHY: BETHANY S. REYNOLDS AND WILLIAM W. REYNOLDS

Library of Congress Cataloging-in-Publication Data
Reynolds, Bethany S.
     Stack-n-whackier quilts / Bethany S. Reynolds.
       p. cm.
     ISBN 1-57432-776-3
     1. Patchwork--Patterns. 2. Kaleidoscope quilts. 3. Rotary cutting.
     4. Machine appliqué. I. Title.
     TT835 .R4592   2001
      746.46'041--dc21
                  2001004039

Additional copies of this book may be ordered from the American Quilter's Society, PO Box 3290, Paducah, KY 42002-3290, or online at www.AQSquilt.com.

Copyright © 2001, Bethany S. Reynolds

DEDICATION

This book is for my students, and for the enthusiastic fans of Stack-n-Whack™ quiltmaking who have asked me, "What's next?" I hope you enjoy exploring these new projects as much as I have enjoyed designing them.

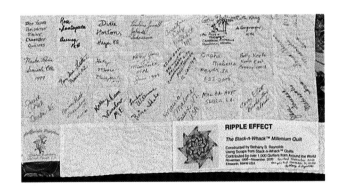

RIPPLE EFFECT, by the author. This quilt incorporates scraps from Stack-n-Whack quilts contributed by more than 1,000 quilters. The backing is pieced from their signature squares, representing all 50 U.S. states and 16 countries.

ACKNOWLEDGMENTS

I am indebted to Meredith Schroeder and the staff at AQS for their support and commitment to excellence. My editor, Barbara Smith, has my special thanks for working with me through three books while maintaining her tact and good humor. Helen Squire deserves special recognition for her tireless efforts to introduce quilters around the world to Stack-n-Whack.

The directions for these projects benefited from the generous efforts of my "Quilt Lab Rats." Sandy Mercado and Ann Czompo, in particular, went above and beyond the call of duty. My dear friends Kathleen Cravens, Eleanor Guthrie, and Ellie Carlisle also came through for me again, and again, and again...thanks, gang!

I am very grateful to Pfaff American Sales for providing me with one of their wonderful machines to piece and quilt my samples. I also thank the manufacturers who contributed materials for the quilts, especially Quilters Dream Cotton™; P&B Textiles; Hi-Fashion Fabrics, Inc.; Robert Kaufman Co.; Hoffman California Fabrics; Kona Bay Fabrics; RJR Fabrics; Free Spirit; Superior Threads; and J.T. Trading Corporation.

Many thanks to Sara Nephew, who contributed her special angle on Stack-n-Whack with her Frozen Roses design, adapted here as SARA'S ROSES.

Karen Combs offered perceptive suggestions for several of the designs. I am thankful for her sound advice, and even more so for her friendship.

My deepest gratitude goes to my husband, Bill, and son, Sam, for their love and patience.

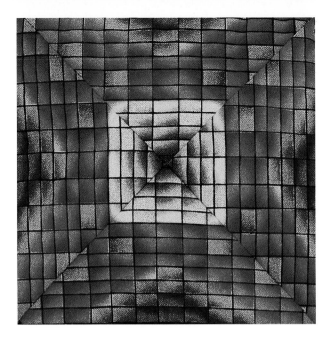

CONTENTS

INTRODUCTION

Are you ready for an adventure into uncharted territory? Within almost every print fabric lies a world of designs waiting to be discovered. With the instructions and projects in this book, you will be ready to find unique and wonderful patterns in the most unexpected places. Whether you are a new quilter looking for an easy but intriguing project or a veteran seeking new challenges, you will find delightful possibilities. The Stack-n-Whack method engages your eyes and mind through each step of the process, from cutting to piecing to finishing, as new designs emerge and change like patterns in a kaleidoscope.

Begin your journey in Part One, which details the Stack-n-Whack method. You will find suggestions for choosing appropriate fabrics and supplies, and a step-by-step explanation of the cutting process.

Part Two contains several basic projects. If you are new to the Stack-n-Whack method, start with one of these quilts. These designs can be made from a wide range of fabrics, and they are suitable for beginning and intermediate quilters. Each quilt features a little something extra – a three-dimensional illusion, for instance, or a bit of appliqué.

Part Three offers three projects especially designed for the Mirror-Image Trick, including a beautiful pieced butterfly quilt. This variation on the basic Stack-n-Whack method creates some exciting effects, with no additional effort in cutting and piecing.

Once you have learned the basic Stack-n-Whack method, you will be ready for the designs in Part Four. The techniques introduced in this section provide a little more control over the finished block design. You will see how to Stack-n-Select to selectively cut identical pieces efficiently and accurately. You can show off your novelty prints in a lighthearted wall quilt or you can make a special border stripe really shine in a classic setting.

Part Five contains general instructions for rotary cutting and machine appliqué, tips for better piecing and pressing, and directions for finishing your quilt with a binding and a hanging sleeve. In addition to the quilting notes that accompany each project, you will find some general quilting suggestions in this section.

You have all your directions in hand, and your guide is ready. Gather your supplies and join us on this exciting quilting quest!

detail SARA'S ROSES

PART ONE:

Stack-n-Whack™ Basics

The Stack-n-Whack method is an easy way to create blocks with unique kaleidoscope designs. These designs require a set of identical pieces cut from a print fabric. Rather than finding and cutting each piece individually, a quilter can cut and layer a number of large, identical print rectangles to make a stack. Each triangle cut from the stack produces a block kit, a set of identical pieces that will create the kaleidoscope effect for one block.

Here is a short overview of the method. The photo tutorial, beginning on page 13, details the process step by step.

1. Cut a rectangle of fabric. This rectangle will generally be about half the width of the fabric, and one or more pattern repeats long, as specified in the directions for each project.

2. Use this first piece to cut additional identical layers. The number of layers needed depends on the number of identical pieces in the block. For example, a hexagon requires six layers, while an octagon requires eight.

3. Stack and carefully pin the layers so that all the motifs in the print line up through the stack.

4. Using the directions for your project, whack the block kits, cutting through all the layers at once.

Selecting Fabric for Stack-n-Whack

Main Fabric

The main fabric is the one that forms the kaleidoscope effect. This fabric sets the tone for the finished quilt. Most medium- to large-scale prints will produce interesting Stack-n-Whack designs (Plates 1–3).

Plate 1. Fabric sample and detail showing block made from fabric.

Plate 2. Fabric sample and detail of SARA'S ROSES.

Plate 3. Fabric sample and detail of MEADOW FLOWERS.

Small-scale prints lack impact when cut into large pieces. However, these prints can be effective in smaller blocks (Plate 4).

Look for prints with good contrast. Lively prints with a variety of shapes, lines, and colors make the most interesting blocks (Plate 5).

Strong contrast or bright colors in the print will make bold kaleidoscope designs (Plate 6).

If you prefer a quieter look, choose a print with medium contrast (Plate 7).

Hand-printed fabrics, such as batiks, are not usually suitable for Stack-n-Whack. The design repeats are not as consistent as the repeats on commercial prints. Save these special fabrics for other projects (Plate 8).

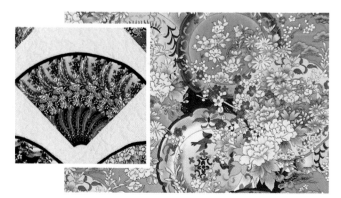

Plate 4. Small prints look best in small blocks.

Plate 6. High-contrast prints produce bold blocks.

Plate 5. Intricate prints like this can create a fascinating variety of blocks.

Plate 7. For more subtle effects, choose a print with lower contrast.

Special effects are possible with certain types of prints. See pages 50-51 for tips on choosing fabrics for the Magic Mirror-Image Trick. Stack-n-Select, on pages 72-79, includes information on working with novelty prints, stripes, and symmetrical prints.

To purchase the correct amount of yardage for a project, you will need to know the length of the design repeat of the main fabric. To determine this length, find a motif along one selvage. Glance along the selvage until you find the same motif, in the same orientation, again. Measure between these two points to find the design repeat length (Plate 9).

Note that the repeat is always measured from the edge of a motif to the same edge of that motif. For example, if you are using a leaf as a reference point and you begin measuring on the left side of the leaf, measure to the left side of the next leaf. If you measure to the right side of the next leaf, you will get an incorrect length.

Plate 8. Hand-printed fabrics are not consistent enough for Stack-n-Whack.

Plate 9. Measure the design repeat length.

Background and Accent Fabrics

These fabrics should complement the main print without competing for attention with the kaleidoscope designs. Because the main fabric may reveal a lot of surprises when cut into block kits, it is difficult to predict the suitability of a particular background. If possible, cut the pieces for at least some of the blocks and lay them out on various backgrounds, arranging them as if they were sewn.

Watch out for distracting background fabric. If you suspect a print may be too busy when you look at the yardage, trust your judgment (Plates 10a–b).

Stripes, plaids, and other directional fabrics can also detract from the Stack-n-Whack designs. Good choices for backgrounds include subtle, low-contrast fabrics with few colors, and monoprints. Mottled textural prints like those shown in Plates 11a–b are always safe choices.

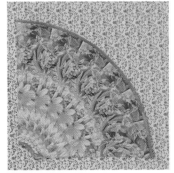

Plates 10a–b. Watch for distracting backgrounds.

Plates 11a–b. Select subtle background fabric.

Black or very dark backgrounds provide a dramatic setting for dark-ground prints (Plates 12a–b).

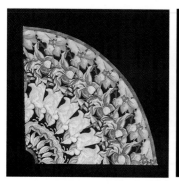 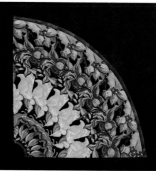

Plates 12a–b. Add drama with a dark background.

Follow the same guidelines for selecting an accent fabric. If the accent fabric appears only in a straight border, you can consider a stripe or other directional fabric. You may want to postpone selecting an accent fabric until you can see its effect with the kaleidoscope blocks.

Supplies for Stack-n-Whack

The supplies you'll need for these projects are quite basic, and you may already have them on hand. If not, you'll find them readily available at most quilt shops or through mail-order quilt suppliers. (See Sources, page 135.)

Here are the essentials:

Rotary cutter. A 45mm or larger blade is essential. If your blade is dull or nicked, treat yourself to a new blade before you start a project. You will be able to cut faster and more accurately and with much less effort. The extra-large (60mm) cutters make cutting multiple layers even easier.

Self-healing rotary cutting mat. Mats come in many configurations, but you'll want one that will allow you to cut across a folded width of fabric without having to shift the fabric. A mat 17" x 23" is the minimum practical size for the projects. A 24" x 36" or larger size will be a little more efficient and will reduce the chance of damaging your tabletop if you get too enthusiastic when you cut.

Rotary cutting rulers. A quality, precision-made ruler is a key ingredient for successful quiltmaking. Some of the projects in this book require a ruler with a 30- or 60-degree angle line, and several use a 45-degree line. Look for rulers with clearly marked ⅛" lines and angle lines that run in both directions. A long rectangular ruler (6" x 24") and a smaller rectangular (6" x 12") or square ruler (6" x 6") are especially useful. For some projects, specialty rulers can make the cutting process easier. See pages 107–114 for more information on rulers and rotary cutting.

You may find these supplies helpful:

Flower-head pins. These are long pins with flat heads. They are useful for pinning a stack, because they will allow the ruler to lie flat for cutting strips. If you do not have these, you can use pins with very small metal heads. But watch out because these are harder to see and may turn up under your cutting blade.

Shall I prewash the fabric?

I have found that prewashing can distort the fabric design, making it more difficult to match the repeats. This has been such a common problem for my students that I now advise them against prewashing the main fabric. This suggestion brings waves of relief to some quilters and fits of dismay to others. If you prefer to prewash your fabric, try to make sure it dries evenly without twisting. Press carefully with the lengthwise grain before cutting, and use spray sizing to restore a crisp, smooth finish.

Spray sizing. Spraying your fabrics with sizing or a light spray starch and pressing them dry before you cut your pieces will make them easier to handle and help prevent stretching. A bit of sizing during the final press will give blocks a crisp, neat finish, and it can do wonders for less-than-perfect piecing. Look for these products in the laundry aisle at a supermarket or chain store.

Seam roll. This sausage-shaped, tightly padded fabric tube allows you to press seam allowances open without catching the tip of your iron. Look for seam rolls in stores or from mail-order resources that sell dressmaking and tailoring notions. You can create your own makeshift seam roll by tightly rolling a magazine and covering it with an old hand towel.

Bath towel. Place an old bath towel over your ironing surface when pressing block units and finished blocks. The terry loops hold the fabric in place and help prevent distortion.

Design wall. It is helpful to have a vertical surface on which to preview fabric choices and to keep blocks in position until you're ready to sew them together. If you can place the design wall where you can stand back from it a bit, it will also help you decide on an overall arrangement of blocks. A solid-colored sheet or an inexpensive fuzzy blanket makes a good design wall.

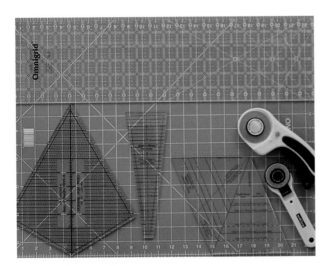

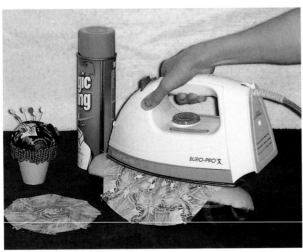

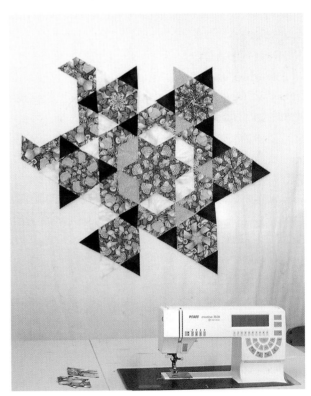

(ABOVE) The author uses an acrylic blanket as a design wall in her studio.

(TOP, LEFT) A selection of basic and specialty cutting supplies.

(BOTTOM, LEFT) Pressing supplies and flower-head pins.

Stack-n-Whack Step by Step

This section outlines the procedure for preparing (stacking) and cutting (whacking) the fabrics to make block kits. While the number of layers and the shapes to cut will vary depending on the design, the stacking process is the same for all projects. Understanding the Stack-n-Whack chart is a key step in using these patterns successfully.

How to Read a Stack-n-Whack Chart

Read this page carefully and refer back to the sample chart as you proceed through the photo tutorial on pages 13–17. Use the top part of the chart, sections A – D, to cut the layers for your stack. After the layers have been stacked, refer to the bottom of the chart, sections E and F, for the whacking instructions.

TOP OF CHART

Section A. At the top of the chart you will find the information on the crosswise measurement of the stack and the number of layers needed for each stack. Most projects call for a 21" width, or about half the crosswise (selvage to selvage) width if the fabric is 42" wide. This width allows for easy and efficient cutting with a 24" ruler. Some projects specify a narrower width to conserve uncut fabric. The number of layers depends on the number of identical pieces needed for each block.

Section B. The first column divides fabric prints into two or more groups, depending on the length of the design repeat. See page 9 for directions on finding this measurement.

Section C. The second column shows how many design repeats to use for each layer, depending on the repeat length. This number of repeats will make the stack long enough to cut the block pieces efficiently.

Section D. The third column shows the number of stacks needed. If you need to make a second stack, use the remaining width of the fabric. Be sure to use a different part of the design for the second stack.

Sample Stack-n-Whack Chart			
A Cut layers 21" wide. Cut 4 identical layers for each stack. Use a different set of identical layers for each additional stack.			
If the lengthwise design repeat is:	Use this many design repeats for each layer:		Make this many stacks:
B 6"–10"	**C** Three repeats		**D** 2
11"–16"	Two repeats		2
Over 16"	One repeat		2
E Whack...		**F** To Make...	
(7) 4" x 21" strips; whack (5) 4" squares from each strip and cut each square once on the diagonal		(67) half-square triangle block kits (10 per strip)	

Top of chart

Bottom of chart

BOTTOM OF CHART

Section E. The left column tells the total number of strips (in parentheses) to cut from one or more stacks, the width of the strips, and the number (in parentheses) and shape of pieces to cut from the strips. Strips are cut crosswise, from the selvage to the torn edge.

Section F. The right column lists the total number of block kits to cut and shows the shape of the block kit.

Finding and Cutting Layers

The repeats are cut from a single layer of fabric. The Stack-n-Whack chart for each project will provide the recommended stack width (section A on the sample chart). If the project directions call for a 21"-wide stack, fold the fabric with selvages together to find the center, or measure 21" from one selvage. For narrower pieces, measure the specified width, which includes the selvage. Cut or tear along the lengthwise grain for about a yard. Fold the remaining fabric out of the way and square off the cut end of the fabric (Plate 13).

Switch the bulk of the fabric to your right if you are right-handed or to your left if you are left-handed. Smooth out the squared-off end of the fabric on your cutting mat. If you have not yet measured the design repeat length, do this now (Plate 14). See page 9 for instructions.

Check the Stack-n-Whack chart for your project and look at the first column (B on the sample chart) to find the length of the repeat. The second column (C on the sample chart) specifies the number of repeats needed for each layer. If the chart shows just one repeat, you will use the length you have just measured for the length of the rectangle. If the chart shows two or three repeats, count out that number of repeats and measure the total length. Use two rulers butted together if necessary. This length is the "magic number." It may be anywhere from 6" to 36", depending on the print and the project. Use this number for the length of the

Plate 13. Square one end of fabric.

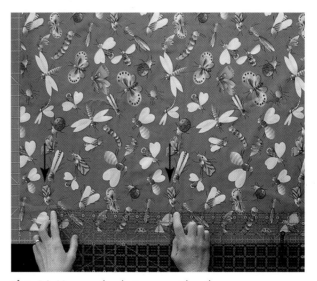

Plate 14. Measure the design repeat length.

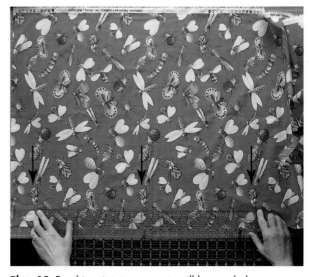

Plate 15. For this print, two repeats will be needed.

cut

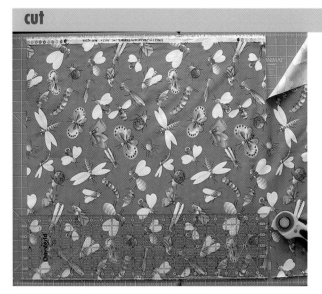

Plate 16. On both sides measure from the squared-off edge to the "magic number" and mark with cuts.

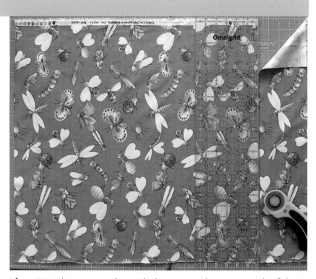

Plate 17. Align your ruler with the cuts and cut across the fabric.

Plate 18. Use your fingers to align the design across the cut edge. The edge will nearly disappear as it lines up.

Plate 19. Cut the second layer along the matched edge.

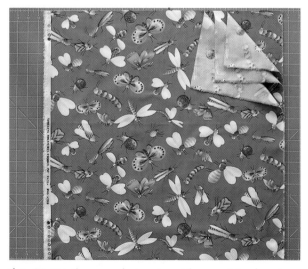

Plate 20. Use the second piece to cut the remaining layers.

rectangle. For the print shown here, the sample chart calls for two repeats, and the magic number is 23¼" (Plate 15, page 13).

For the next step, ignore the print motifs. It no longer matters what part of the print you used as a reference to find the repeat length. Place the ruler along the selvage with the magic number at the squared-off edge. Mark the length with a 4"–6" cut at the other end of the ruler. Measure and cut again at the torn side (Plate 16).

Align your ruler with the cut marks and cut across the width to make the first layer (Plate 17).

With selvages and cut edges aligned, lay the first rectangle on the remaining fabric so that the print matches. Smooth out the top layer and use your fingertips to match up the design all across the cut edge. The edge should nearly disappear as it lines up with the print on the lower, uncut layer. The other end of the rectangle does not need to match up precisely (Plate 18).

When you have matched the top layer, lay your ruler down along the matched edge and cut across (Plate 19).

You now have two identical print rectangles. Set the top piece aside. Cut or tear along the length of the fabric, if necessary, and smooth the portion you will be cutting. Use the second layer to cut a third layer and the remaining layers. The second layer will be the correct length, even if you made a minor error in measuring or cutting the first layer. By using the second piece as a guide to cut the rest, you will not compound any errors. You will still be able to use the first layer in the stack, even if it is slightly shorter or longer than the others.

Repeat this process until you have the number of layers needed for the stack (Plate 20).

Stacking the Layers

Press the layers one at a time to remove any wrinkles, pressing along the lengthwise grain to avoid distortion. If you have prewashed the fabric, it is a good idea to use a little sizing or spray starch to return some crispness to the fabric. This will make the pieces easier to handle and will help keep bias edges from stretching.

Stack the layers, smoothing each piece so that the selvages align. When you have all the layers stacked, use the following "stick-pinning" method to line up the motifs accurately through the layers. You'll need one pin with a large round head, and several flower-head pins. These are long pins with a large flat head that will not interfere with the ruler. If you do not have these, you can use long pins with small metal heads. They are harder to see, though, so take extra care to keep stray pins out of the way of your cutting blade.

Why do I use lengthwise repeats?

Be sure to cut all the layers for the stack from the same half of the fabric. Printing and finishing processes can cause slight distortions even in high quality fabrics, and the differences may be noticeable in the finished blocks if you use crosswise, rather than lengthwise, repeats. You may also find that the crosswise repeats are staggered, so that they only match up for part of the width, resulting in a stack that is too narrow to cut enough block kits for your project.

To "stick-pin" fabric layers, select a point on the fabric design about 1"–1½" from the crosswise (cut) edge. Look for something that's distinctive and easy to spot, such as the tip of a leaf or in this case, a bug's foot. Place the point of the round-headed pin on this spot (Plate 21).

Lift the top layer of fabric, sliding the pin through. Find the same point on the next layer and slide the pin through (Plate 22).

Continue until you have stuck the pin through all the layers.

Slide the pin all the way through to the head and hold it in place with your thumb and forefinger. Hold the pin straight up and down and smooth out the surrounding fabric. Take a flower-head pin and pin across through all the layers, right beside the stick pin (Plate 23).

Remove the stick pin. Lay the fabric down flat and repeat this at three other points across the width. For additional accuracy, also pin 5"–6" up along the selvage and torn edge (Plate 24).

stack

Plate 21. Place the pin on a distinctive part of the design.

Plate 22. Put the pin through the same spot on all the layers.

Plate 23. Hold the pin and fabric layers tight. Use a flower-head pin to pin through all layers.

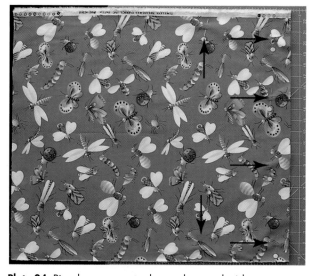

Plate 24. Pin along one cut edge and on each side.

Whacking the Block Kits

The strip cutting method shown here produces random, unplanned kaleidoscope effects. To selectively cut the block kits, see the Stack-n-Select instructions beginning on page 72.

Trim the stack along the pinned crosswise edge to ensure a straight edge through all the layers (Plate 25).

Turn the stack around or rotate the mat. Cut a strip through all the layers, using the strip-width measurement given in the Stack-n-Whack chart for your project (Plate 26).

Cut the strip into block kits, removing pins as you go to protect the rotary-cutter blade (Plate 27). Instructions are included for rotary cutting other basic shapes (pages 107–114).

For more accurate cutting, repin the crosswise edge before cutting each additional strip.

Making Additional Stacks

If the project requires a second stack (section D on the sample chart), cut the stack from the remaining width of the fabric, starting with a new first layer. This stack should produce a new assortment of blocks. If the crosswise repeats line up side by side, trim an inch or two from the beginning of the fabric to offset the pattern before cutting the first layer.

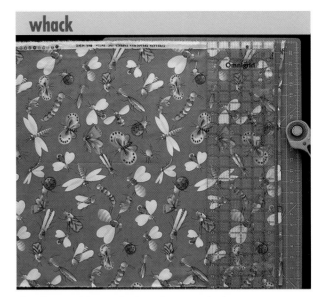

Plate 25. Trim the stack along the pinned edge.

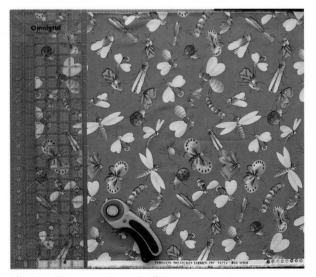

Plate 26. Cut a strip through all layers.

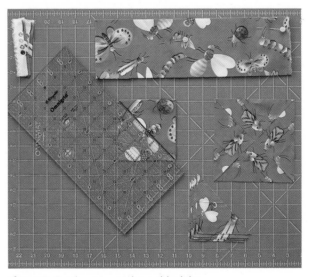

Plate 27. Cut the strip stack into block kits.

PART TWO:

Quilt Plans to
Stack-n-Whack

detail SECRET STAIRWAYS

SECRET STAIRWAYS
40" x 44", made by the author.

detail SECRET STAIRWAYS

SECRET STAIRWAYS

Finished Quilt Top: 40" x 44"
Finished Block: 6¼"

Intermediate

Are we looking down at stairs or up at boxes looming overhead? In any case, careful fabric selection can enhance the illusion. For the four accent fabrics, choose two values in each of two color families. In each block, the two lighter fabrics (one from each color family) are in opposite corners, and the two darker fabrics are in the other two corners. A black print can add a dramatic accent when used as the darker value of one color, as in the SECRET STAIRWAYS quilt where it serves as the dark side of the red boxes.

Fabric Requirements					
Measurements in yards unless otherwise indicated.					
If the design repeat of **Main Fabric A** is	6"–10"	11"–14"	15"–20"	21"–27"	over 27"
You will need this many yards	3½	3¼	4¾	3¼	4 repeats
Additional Fabrics					
Accents B, C, D, and E	⅜ each of 4 colors				
Outer Border	⅜ pieced or 1¼ seamless				
Backing	2⅝ pieced lengthwise				
Binding – cut 2½" strips crosswise	½				

Cutting Main Fabric A

Prepare the main fabric, following the directions on pages 12–17. See page 108 for general instructions on cutting half-square triangles. Check the block kits for accuracy by using the guide on page 123.

Stack-n-Whack Chart for Secret Stairways Quilt		
Cut layers 21" wide. Cut 4 identical layers for each stack. Use a different set of identical layers for each additional stack.		
If the lengthwise design repeat is:	Use this many design repeats for each layer:	Make this many stacks*:
6"–10"	Three repeats	1
11"–16"	Two repeats	1
Over 16"	One repeat	1
Whack...		To Make...
(4) 4" strips; whack (5) 4" squares from each strip and cut each square once on the diagonal		(40) half-square triangle block kits (10 per strip)
* Make two stacks if you wish to selectively cut some of the block kits. See Part Four for more information.		

Cutting Accent Fabric Triangles	
From each fabric, cut...	Cut strips into...
(2) 4" strips across width	(20) 4" squares (10 per strip); cut each square once on the diagonal to make (40) half-square triangles of each fabric

Piecing the Square Block Units

Each stack of 4 identical triangles is a block kit (Fig. 2–1). Place 2 triangles from 1 block kit right sides together. Sew them together on one short side. Repeat with the second pair of triangles. This is one set (Figs. 2–2 and 2–3).

Piece all the block kits into sets of pairs. If you chain piece these, clip the chain between each set of pairs to keep the matching pairs together (Fig. 2–4).

Sew the pairs together to make square units. As you match up the pairs, flip the seam allowances in opposite directions so they nest together at the center. Finger-crease the center allowances to one side (Figs. 2–5 and 2–6).

Sew a triangle of Fabric B (your lightest accent fabric) to each square unit, centering the triangle along one edge (Fig. 2–7).

Sew a triangle of Fabric C (lighter shade of the second color) to the opposite side of each square unit, centering the triangle along the edge (Fig. 2–8). Finger crease the allowances toward the accent triangles (Fig. 2–9).

Turn the block units so that the B triangle (first fabric added) is at the top. Sew a Fabric D triangle (the darker shade of the first color added) to the right side of each square unit, centering the triangle on the square (Fig. 2–10).

Turn the units and sew a Fabric E triangle (the darker shade of the second color) to the opposite edge (Fig. 2–11). Press seam allowances toward the accent triangles (Fig. 2–12). Piece 25 units.

Piecing the Partial Block Units

Piece 15 more block kits into squares. Referring to the quilt assembly diagram, add accent triangles to 2 or 3 sides of the square centers to make the blocks on the outside edges. Follow the diagram carefully. There are several different units.

Assembling Secret Stairways

Arrange the blocks according to the quilt assembly diagram. Trim 8 of the partial blocks as shown, placing the ruler edge ¼" from the

Piecing the Blocks

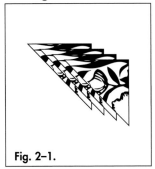

Fig. 2–1.

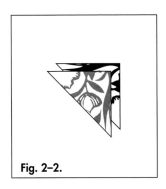

Fig. 2–2.

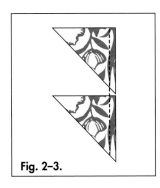

Fig. 2–3.

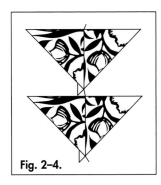

Fig. 2–4.

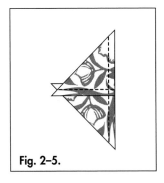

Fig. 2–5.

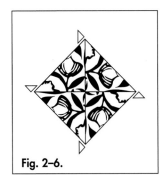

Fig. 2–6.

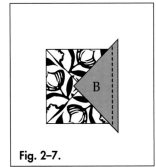

Fig. 2–7.

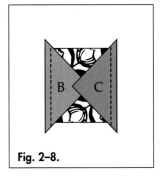

Fig. 2–8.

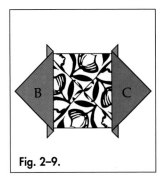

Fig. 2–9.

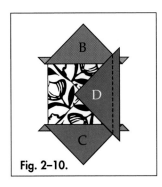

Fig. 2–10.

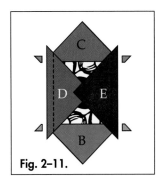

Fig. 2–11.

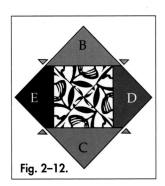

Fig. 2–12.

tips to leave a seam allowance (Figs. 2–13 and 2–14).

Place individual accent triangles along the sides as indicated in the assembly diagram to complete the pattern. Sew the seams in each diagonal row, then sew the diagonal rows together.

Adding the Borders

There will be many bias edges on the quilt top. Take care not to stretch them when measuring and sewing the borders. Notice that the quilt, as pictured, is wider than it is long, and the borders have butted corners. From the border fabric, cut five 2½" strips across width or cut four 2½" x 42" lengthwise strips. For borders cut across the width, piece the strips together into 1 long strip before cutting the border lengths. With the top lying flat, mea-

sure the quilt top across the center and cut 2 border strips this length. Pin the strips to the top and bottom of the quilt, matching the centers and ends. Sew the border strips, easing the bias edges as necessary. Measure the length of the quilt through the center, including borders, and cut 2 border strips this length. Pin and sew them to the sides of the quilt, easing the bias edges as necessary.

Finishing the Quilt

Prepare the backing by cutting the yardage in half and sewing the pieces together length-wise. Layer the quilt top, batting, and backing. Quilt the layers and bind the raw edges.

Quilting Notes

SECRET STAIRWAYS is quilted in the seam lines for a crisp geometric effect.

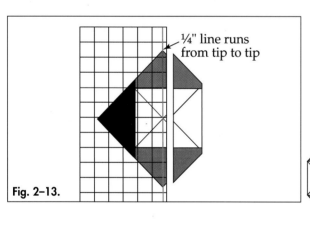

Fig. 2–13.

¼" line runs from tip to tip

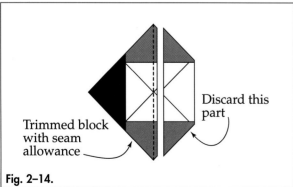

Trimmed block with seam allowance

Discard this part

Fig. 2–14.

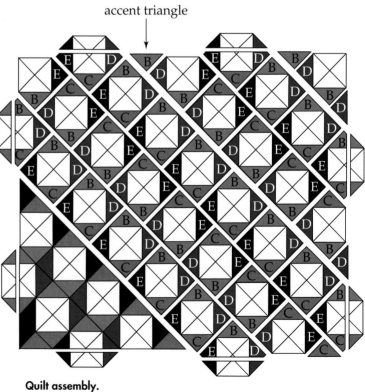

accent triangle

Quilt assembly.

TREASURE BOXES

46½" x 53½", made by the author.

detail TREASURE BOXES

TREASURE BOXES

Finished Quilt Top: 46½" x 53½
Finished Block: 5"

Intermediate

More optical fun! These little boxes are a snap to piece. Choose two values of a single color for the box sides to enhance the three-dimensional effect. Make sure the background fabric contrasts well with both the main fabric and the box fabrics.

Fabric Requirements					
Measurements in yards unless otherwise indicated.					
If the design repeat of **Main Fabric A** is	6"–10"	11"–14"	15"–20"	21"–27"	over 27"
You will need this many yards	2½	2½	2½	3½	4 repeats
Additional Fabrics					
Background B	1¾				
Accents C and D – box sides	½ each of 2 colors				
Border	½ pieced or 1⅝ seamless				
Backing – pieced crosswise	3				
Binding – cut 2½" strips crosswise	½				

Cutting Main Fabric A

Prepare the main fabric, following the directions on pages 12–17. See page 109 for general instructions on cutting quarter-square triangles. Check the block kits for accuracy by using the guide on page 130.

Stack-n-Whack Chart for Treasure Boxes Quilt

Cut layers 17" wide. Cut 4 identical layers for each stack.
Use a different set of identical layers for each additional stack.

If the lengthwise design repeat is:	Use this many design repeats for each layer:	Make this many stacks:
6"–10"	Two repeats	2
11"–21"	One repeat	2
Over 21"	One repeat	1

Whack...	To Make...
(4) 5¼" strips; whack (3) 5¼" squares from each strip and cut each square twice on the diagonal	(42) quarter-square triangle block kits (12 per strip) ▶

Cutting Background Fabric B

Position in Quilt	First Cut	Second Cut	Third Cut
Block Corners	(3) 1½" strips across width	(84) 1½" squares	
Alternate Blocks	(5) 5½" strips across width	(30) 5½" squares	
Side Triangles	(2) 8⅜" strips across width	(6) 8⅜" squares	Cut each square twice on the diagonal to make (22) quarter-square triangles
Corner Triangles	(1) 4½" x 9" strip	(2) 4½" squares	Cut each square once on the diagonal to make (4) half-square triangles

Cutting Box Fabrics C and D

First Cut	Second Cut
(2) 6" strips across the width from each fabric	(42) 1½" x 6" rectangles from each fabric

Piecing the Treasure Boxes Blocks

Piece 42 Treasure Boxes blocks as follows:

To prepare the box sides, place a square of Background Fabric B at one end of each box fabric rectangle, right sides together. Sew across the square in the direction shown (Fig. 2–15, page 26).

Trim the seam allowances to ¼". Press them toward the triangle (Fig. 2–16, page 26).

For the main fabric, each stack of 4 identical half-square triangles is a block kit (Fig. 2–17, page 26).

Place 2 triangles from one block kit right sides together. Piece together on one short side.

Repeat with the second pair of triangles in the kit. This is one set of pairs (Figs. 2–18 and 2–19).

Piece the block kits into sets of pairs. You can chain piece these. Clip the chain between each set of pairs to keep the matching pairs together (Fig. 2–20).

Place 2 matching pairs together, matching the seams at the center and finger-pressing the seam allowances in opposite directions. Stitch

part way down, stopping about 1½" below the center seam (Fig. 2–21).

With the pieced square wrong side up, place a rectangle of Fabric C (right side up) under the right edge as shown. (The triangle of Fabric B is at the top of the rectangle.) Stitch down the length of the triangle (Fig. 2–22).

Finger-press the seam allowances toward the main fabric square. Turn the square right

Piecing the Blocks

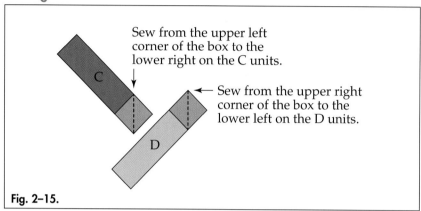

Sew from the upper left corner of the box to the lower right on the C units.

Sew from the upper right corner of the box to the lower left on the D units.

Fig. 2–15.

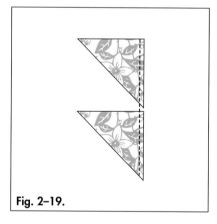

Fig. 2–16.

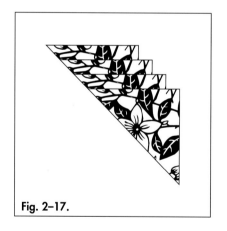

Fig. 2–17.

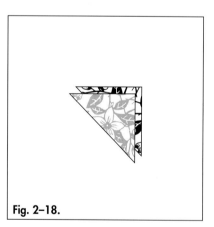

Fig. 2–18.

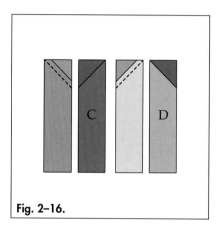

Fig. 2–19.

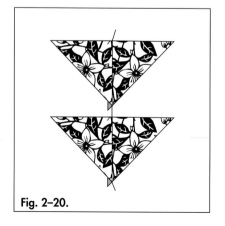

Fig. 2–20.

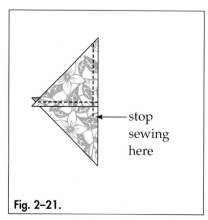

stop sewing here

Fig. 2–21.

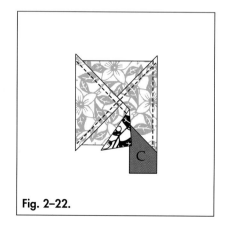

Fig. 2–22.

side up. Sew a rectangle of Fabric D to the right edge as shown, right sides together (Figs. 2–23 and 2–24).

Finger-press the seam allowances toward the D rectangle. Fold the triangles, right sides together as shown, with the seams nesting together and the straight edges together (Fig. 2–25).

Trim the excess fabric from C and D to create a straight line along the bias edge. To do this accurately, place the edge of the ruler on the edge with the partial seam, and the 45-degree ruler line on the edge of the rectangular strip as shown (Fig. 2–26). Then finish sewing the partial seam (Fig. 2–27).

Press the seam allowances to one side. Trim off the triangle tips to complete the block. (Fig. 2–28).

Piecing the Blocks (cont.)

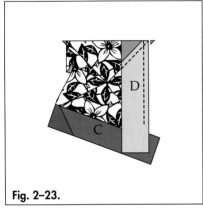

Fig. 2–23.

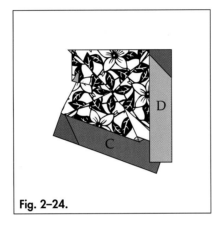

Fig. 2–24.

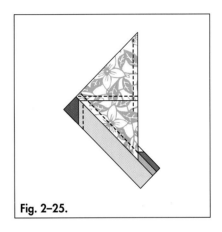

Fig. 2–25.

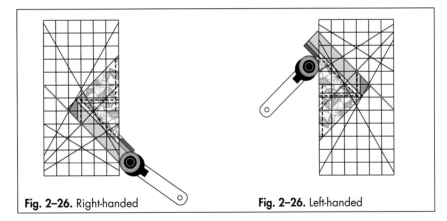

Fig. 2–26. Right-handed   Fig. 2–26. Left-handed

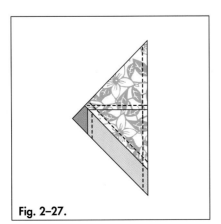

Fig. 2–27.

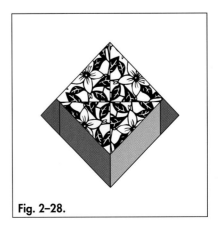

Fig. 2–28.

Assembling the Quilt

Arrange the pieced blocks according to the quilt assembly diagram. Add the unpieced alternate blocks, corners, and side triangles of Fabric B. Sew the seams in each diagonal row, then sew the diagonal rows together.

Adding the Borders

The borders have butted corners. Cut (5) 2½" strips across the width or cut (4) 2½" x 53" lengthwise strips. For borders cut across the width, piece the strips together into one long strip before cutting the border strips to length. Measure the quilt top down the center and cut two border strips this length. Sew the strips to the long sides. Measure across the width in the center of the quilt, including borders, and cut two border strips this length. Sew them to the top and bottom.

Finishing the Quilt

Prepare the backing by piecing together two 1½-yard lengths of backing fabric. Layer the quilt top, batting, and backing. Quilt the layers and bind the raw edges.

Quilting Notes

Quilting lines run through each vertical column of boxes in the seam lines. A second set of quilting lines forms a triangle on each box top, crossing through each box top on the horizontal seam line and continuing around the seam lines between the main fabric and the box side fabrics. In the background, quilting outlines each box about ¼" from the seams. The background areas are filled with free-motion vines and leaves.

Quilt assembly.

MEADOW FLOWERS
54" x 57", made by the author.

detail MEADOW FLOWERS

MEADOW FLOWERS

Finished Quilt Top: 54" x 57"
Finished Blocks: 9" x 16", 9" x 6", and
9" x 10"

Intermediate

S ow bright wildflowers, each one unique! This design requires just three repeats of the main fabric. Simple appliqué complements the pieced Stack-n-Whack blossoms. For general instructions on machine appliqué, see page 116.

Fabric Requirements					
Measurements in yards unless otherwise indicated.					
If the design repeat of **Main Fabric A** is	6"–10"	11"–14"	15"–20"	21"–27"	over 27"
You will need this many yards	⅞	1¼	1¾	2⅜	3 repeats

Additional Fabrics	
Background and Second Border – pieced	2⅜
Appliqué Fabric – leaves, stems, and calyxes	¾
Accent – First and Third Borders – pieced	½
Backing – pieced crosswise	3½
Binding – cut 2½" strips crosswise	½
Optional – Scraps of novelty print for butterfly appliqué	

Cutting Main Fabric A

Prepare the main fabric, following the directions on page 12–17. See pages 110–111 for general instructions on cutting 45-degree triangles. Check the block kits for accuracy using the guide on page 126.

Stack-n-Whack Chart for Meadow Flowers Quilt		
Cut layers 21" wide. Cut 3 identical layers for each stack. Use a different set of identical layers for each additional stack.		
If the lengthwise design repeat is:	Use this many design repeats for each layer:	Make this many stacks:
6"–12"	One repeat	2
Over 12"	One repeat	1
Whack...		**To Make...**
(2) 5½" strips; whack 45° triangle wedges		(12) 45° triangle block kits (6 per strip) ▲

Cutting Background Fabric		
First Cut	**Second Cut**	**Third Cut**
(1) 6" strip across width	(12) 6" 45° triangle wedges	Cut each wedge up the center to make (12) left and (12) right half-wedges
(1) 3½" strip across width	(12) 3½" squares	Cut each square once on the diagonal to make (24) half-square triangles
(1) 6½" strip across width	(3) 6½" x 9½" rectangles	
(3) 2" strips across width	(12) 2" x 9½" rectangles	
(4) 3" x 53" lengthwise strips	Set aside for second border	
From the remaining width of fabric – approximately 30" – cut:		
(5) 10½" strips across width	(15) 9½" x 10½" rectangles	

Cutting First and Third Borders
Cut (10) 1½" strips across the width; piece the strips together into one long strip

Piecing the Meadow Flower Blocks

Piece 12 flower blossom units as follows:

Each stack of three identical wedges is a block kit.

With right sides together, piece a pair of wedges from one block kit (Figs. 2–29 and 2–30).

Finger-press the seam allowances open (Fig. 2–31). Add the third wedge to the pair and finger-press the seam allowances open (Figs. 2–32 and 2–33).

Add a half-wedge of background fabric to each long side as shown. Press the seam allowances toward the background (Figs. 2–34, 2–35, 2–36, and 2–37). Trim the triangle tips. Add half-square triangles of background fabric to the corners as shown (Figs. 2–38 and 2–39).

Sew a 9½" x 10½" rectangle to the bottom of each flower-blossom unit. Sew a 2" x 9½" rectangle to the top of each flower-blossom unit (Fig. 2–40).

Piecing the Blocks

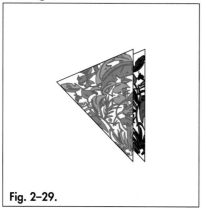

Fig. 2–29.

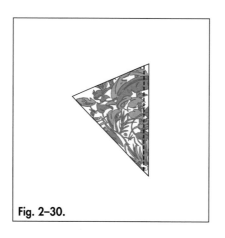

Fig. 2–30.

Fig. 2–31.

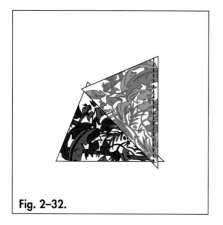

Fig. 2–32.

Fig. 2–33.

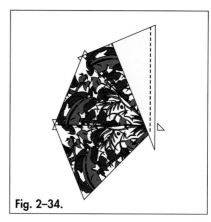

Fig. 2–34.

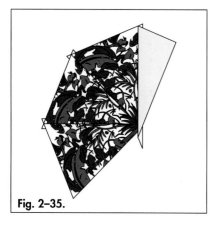

Fig. 2–35.

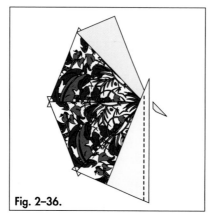

Fig. 2–36.

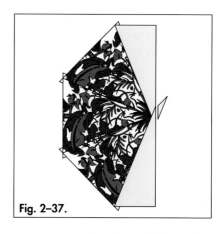

Fig. 2–37.

See page 116 for general instructions for appliqué. You will need 6 bud units cut from scraps of Main Fabric A. From the leaf appliqué fabric cut a total of 90 leaves and 18 calyxes. The patterns for these are on pages 124–126.

For the stems, cut 12 strips ½" x 10", 3 strips ½" x 6", and 3 strips ½" x 4". Use the method of your choice to appliqué the stems, leaves, and calyxes to each tall flower block. The calyx will overlap the seam (Fig. 2–41).

Use the 6½" x 9 ½" rectangles for the 3 two-leaf blocks and the 3 remaining 9½" x 10½" rectangles for the four-leaf blocks (Figs. 2–42 and 2–43).

Assembling the Quilt

Follow the quilt assembly diagram on page 34 to arrange the quilt top. Sew the horizontal seams in each column, then sew the vertical columns together.

For the optional butterfly appliqué, cut butterflies from novelty print fabric and appliqué in place. Add antennae with hand or machine embroidery stitching.

Piecing the Blocks (cont.)

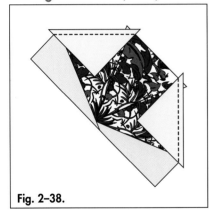

Fig. 2–38.

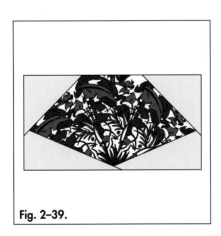

Fig. 2–39.

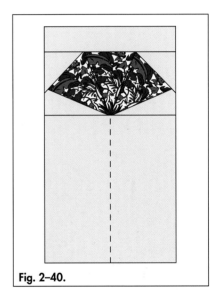

Fig. 2–40.

Fig. 2–41.

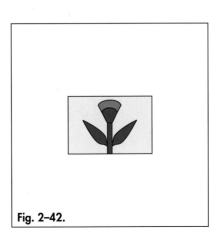

Fig. 2–42.

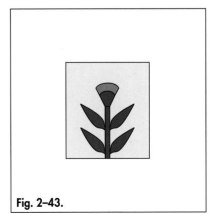

Fig. 2–43.

Adding the Borders

Cut (10) 1½" strips across the width; piece the strips together into one long strip.

The borders have butted corners. Measure the quilt top down the center and cut two border strips this length. Sew the borders to two opposite sides. Measure across the width in the center of the quilt, including borders, and cut two border strips this length. Sew them to the remaining sides.

Repeat for the second border, using the lengthwise strips of background fabric.

Repeat for the third border, using the remaining strips of accent border fabric.

Finishing the Quilt

Prepare the backing by cutting the yardage in half and sewing the pieces together lengthwise. Layer the quilt top, batting, and backing. Quilt the layers and bind the raw edges.

Quilting Notes

The narrow borders are quilted in the seam lines. Each flower is outline quilted about ¼" from the appliqué or seam line. The large blossoms have a little free-motion quilting in a sunburst pattern. The background and wide border are free-motion quilted with continuous spirals.

Quilt assembly.

SARA'S ROSES

55½" x 72½", made by the author.

detail SARA'S ROSES

SARA'S ROSES

Finished Quilt Top: 55½" x 72½"
Finished Hexagon: approx. 16½" x 19"

Intermediate

Diamond and triangle block kits combine in this opulent quilt adapted from a design by Sara Nephew. Sara's original quilt is shown on page 42. The intricate appearance is deceptive because the piecing is really quite easy. The smaller, simplified version, whose pattern is given here, contains just one main fabric. If you would like to experiment with multiple main fabrics, remember that you will need six repeats of each. For the accent triangles, you can play with scraps from your stash as Sara has done. Arrange the pieces on a design wall as you work to plan your fabric placement.

Fabric Requirements					
Measurements in yards unless otherwise indicated.					
If the design repeat of **Main Fabric A** is	7"–10"	11"–14"	15"–17"	18"–27"	over 27"
You will need this many yards	5¼	5	6	5	6 repeats

Additional Fabrics – see block diagram, page 37	
Accent B – triangles surrounding stars in hexagon blocks	¾
Accent C – outer triangles in hexagon blocks	½
Accent D – triangles in triangle blocks	½
Accent E – setting triangles	⅞
Border	¾ pieced or 2 seamless
Backing – pieced crosswise	3½
Binding – cut 2½" strips crosswise	½

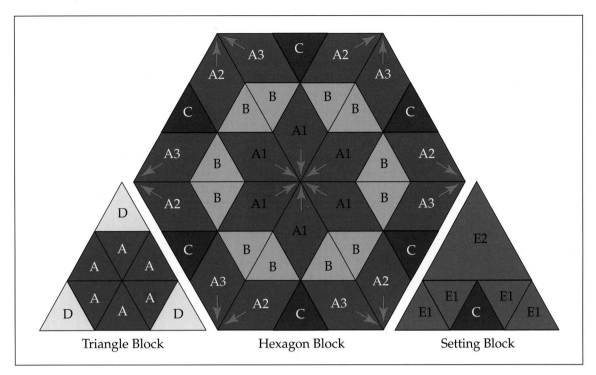

Triangle Block   Hexagon Block   Setting Block

Block diagram.

Cutting Main Fabric A

Prepare the main fabric, following the directions on pages 12–17. See pages 112–113 for general instructions on cutting 60-degree diamonds and triangles. Check block kit for accuracy by using the guide on page 126.

Stack-n-Whack Chart for Sara's Roses Quilt		
Cut layers 21" wide. Cut 6 identical layers for each stack. Use a different set of identical layers for each additional stack.		
If the lengthwise design repeat is:	Use this many design repeats for each layer:	Make this many stacks:
7"–10"	Three repeats	2
11"–20"	Two repeats	2
Over 20"	One repeat	2
Whack...	**To Make...**	
(3) 3½" strips across the width	(18) 60° triangle block kits (8 per strip) ▲	
(6) 3¼" strips across the width	(27) 60° diamond block kits (5 per strip) ◆	

Cutting Accent Fabric		
Fabric and position	**First Cut**	**Second Cut**
B - triangle surrounding stars	(6) 3½" strips across width	(108) 60° triangles – 18 per strip
C - outer triangle in hexagon blocks	(4) 3½" strips across width	(60) 60° triangles – 18 per strip
D - triangles in triangle blocks	(3) 3½" strips across width	(54) 60° triangles – 18 per strip
E1 - small setting triangles	(2) 3½" strips across width	(24) 60° triangles – 18 per strip
E2 - large setting triangles	(1) 6" strip across width	(6) 60° triangles
E3 - top and bottom setting triangles	(2) 5½" strips across width	(6) 9½" x 5½" rectangles*
*Place the rectangles together in pairs, wrong sides together, and cut each pair once on the diagonal. This will make 6 left and 6 right setting triangles.		

Piecing the Hexagon Blocks

Each hexagon block contains 3 different sets of 6 identical diamonds. One set (A1) forms the star in the center of the block, surrounded by Fabric B triangles. The other 2 sets (A2 and A3), in combination with the Fabric C triangles, form a ring around the star. Select combinations for all 9 blocks before beginning to piece. Choose the most interesting kits for the center stars, then choose 2 compatible kits to go with each center.

Working on one block at a time, piece 9 hexagon blocks as follows:

Arrange the A1 diamonds and decide which tip to use in the center (Figs. 2–44a and b).

Place reference pins in the center tip of each diamond (Fig. 2–45).

Place the 6 identical diamonds next to your machine with the ends of the diamonds that will be in the center (the ends with the reference pins) closest to you. Sew a Fabric B triangle to the top right edge of a diamond, with the triangle's straight-grain edge placed as shown by the arrow. The top corner of the triangle should align with the tip of the diamond. The triangle will extend ¼" past the diamond at the lower end. Finger-press the seam allowances toward the triangle (Figs. 2–46 and 2–47).

Repeat for the other five diamonds, then remove the reference pins.

Turn the diamonds and add Fabric B triangles to the opposite sides, again aligning the tip of the triangle with the tip of the diamond (Figs. 2–48 and 2–49).

Carefully press the finished A/B units from the right side, pressing the seam allowances toward the triangles.

Decide which tips of the A2 and A3 diamonds will come together in the corners of the block, as indicated by the arrows in the illustrations. Place reference pins in these tips (Fig. 2–50).

With the reference pin at the bottom, place the straight edge of the triangle as shown, and sew a Fabric C triangle to the top right edge of each A2 diamond. Finger-press the seam allowances toward the diamond (Fig. 2–51 and 2–52).

Sew an A3 diamond, with the reference pin at the bottom, to the Fabric C triangle. Finger-press the seam allowances toward the diamond (Fig. 2–53 and 2–54).

Piece the A/B units to the A/C units as

Piecing the Hexagon Blocks

Fig. 2–44a–b. Decide which tip to use in the center.

Fig. 2–45.

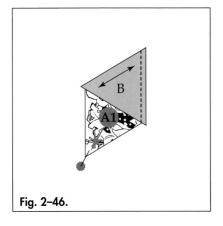

Fig. 2–46.

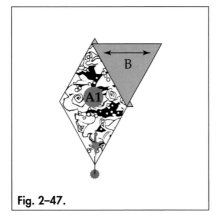

Fig. 2–47.

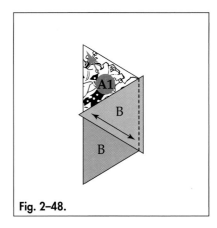

Fig. 2–48.

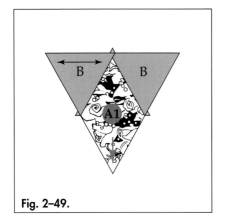

Fig. 2–49.

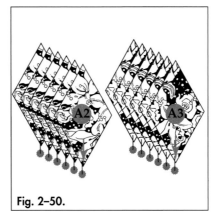

Fig. 2–50.

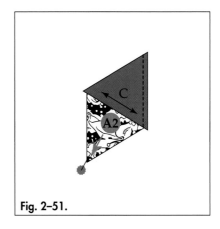

Fig. 2–51.

Fig. 2–52.

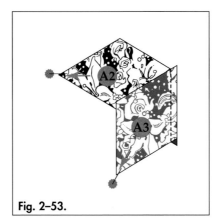

Fig. 2–53.

Fig. 2–54.

shown. Finger-press the seam allowances toward the center on 3 of the units and away from the center on the other 3 units (Fig. 2–55).

Arrange the 6 pieces so that the seam allowances alternate. Make half-hexagons by piecing together a pair of triangles and then adding a third triangle to one side. Finger-press the seam allowances open (Fig. 2–56).

Sew the 2 half-hexagons together to complete each hexagon block. Press the seam allowances open (Fig. 2–57).

Piecing the Triangle & Setting Blocks

Piece 18 Triangle Blocks as follows:

Unpin one block kit (6 identical triangles), taking note of the straight-grain edge. This will be the outside edge of the hexagon, and the opposite point will be the center. To keep from unintentionally turning a triangle, put a reference pin in each of the 6 triangles on the straight edge (Fig. 2–58).

Pick up the first 2 triangles of the set and sew them, right sides together, with the refer-

Piecing the Hexagon Blocks (cont.)

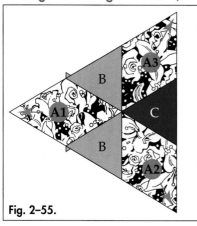

Fig. 2–55.

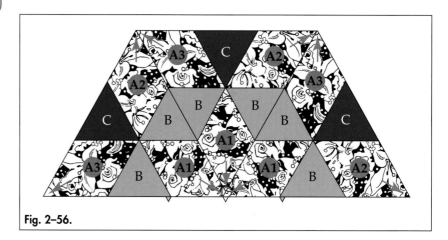

Fig. 2–56.

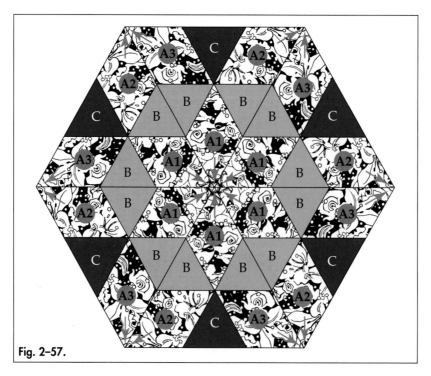

Fig. 2–57.

ence pins at the top left as shown (Fig. 2–59). Repeat with a second pair of triangles. Finger-press these seam allowances open (Fig. 2–60).

Sew one of the remaining triangles to each pair, matching the tips at the top and bottom. The reference pins should be on the same side, as shown. Press these seam allowances open (Figs. 2–61 and 2–62).

You should have two identical halves. Remove the pins. Place the halves right sides together and stitch across the center of the block, matching the crossed seams at the center. Press the seam allowances open (Fig. 2–63).

Add D triangles to every other side of the hexagon. Press the seam allowances toward the triangles (Figs. 2–64 and 2–65).

Use the Fabric C triangles and the small and large Fabric E triangles to piece 6 setting blocks as shown (Figs. 2–66 and 2–67).

Assembling the Quilt

Arrange the blocks and the top and bottom setting triangles according to the quilt assembly diagram. Piece the blocks together in sections, then sew the diagonal seams between the sections.

Piecing the Triangle and Setting Blocks

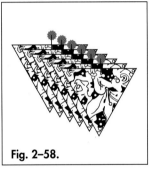

Fig. 2–58.

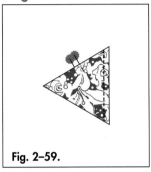

Fig. 2–59.

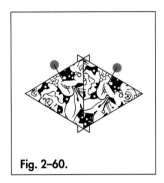

Fig. 2–60.

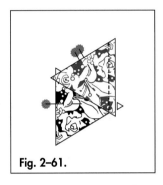

Fig. 2–61.

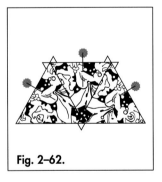

Fig. 2–62.

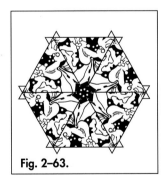

Fig. 2–63.

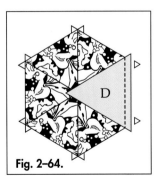

Fig. 2–64.

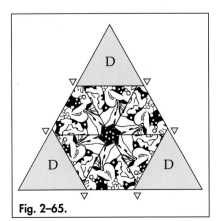

Fig. 2–65.

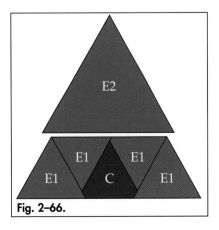

Fig. 2–66.

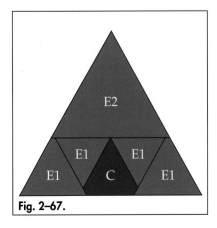

Fig. 2–67.

Adding the Borders

The borders have butted corners. For the border, cut six 3½" strips across the width, or cut four 3½" x 69" lengthwise strips. For borders cut across the width, piece the strips together into one long strip before cutting the border lengths. With the top lying flat, measure it down the center and cut 2 border strips this length. Pin the borders to the long sides, matching the centers and ends. Sew the borders, easing the bias edges as necessary. Measure across the width in the center of the quilt, including borders, and cut 2 border strips this length. Pin and sew them to the top and bottom, easing the bias edges as before.

FROZEN ROSES, 67½" x 95", made by Sara Nephew. Sara cut stacks from several different fabrics for a rich effect.

Quilt assembly.

Finishing the Quilt

Prepare the backing by piecing together two 1¾-yard lengths of backing fabric. Layer the quilt top, batting, and backing. Quilt the layers and bind the raw edges.

Quilting Notes

SARA'S ROSES is quilted in the seam lines between colors with gold metallic thread. Straight-line quilting splits each A1 and A3 diamond lengthwise. Free-motion quilting highlights the kaleidoscope design in each Rose Star and hexagon block, and stippling covers the B and D triangles, the setting triangles, and the border.

FAN QUILT
90" x 107", made by the author.

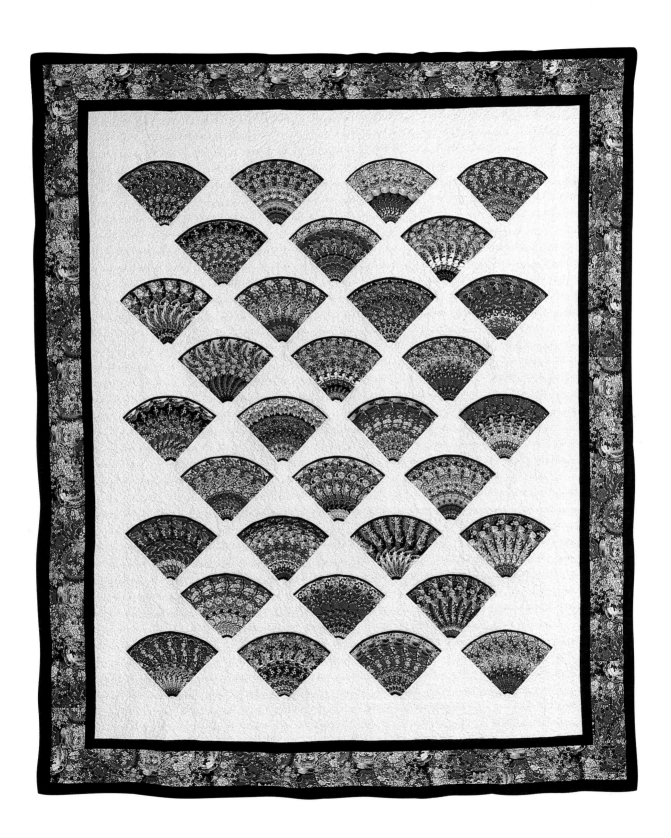

FAN QUILT

Finished Quilt Top: 90" x 107"
Finished Block: 12"

Easy

detail FAN QUILT

The fabric edge trim on these lovely fans is more than a pretty accent. It also provides a simple way to turn the curved raw edges to the back. Easy in-the-ditch, straight-stitch appliqué secures the fans to the background squares. This is a great design to use for Stack-n-Whack experimentation. The Mirror-Image Trick is very effective in the fan block, and it requires no extra fabric. See Part Three, pages 50–51, for instructions on using this method. You can also use the Stack-n-Select method, described in Part Four, to cut the fan wedges from a border stripe or novelty print, as shown in the blocks on pages 72–79. Because selective cutting requires more fabric than basic Stack-n-Whack cutting, be prepared to use more yardage or reduce the number of blocks in your project.

Fabric Requirements					
Measurements in yards unless otherwise indicated.					
If the design repeat of **Main Fabric A** is	6"–10"	11"–14"	15"–17"	18"–27"	over 27"
You will need this many yards	5½	5¼	6¼	5	6 repeats

Additional Fabrics	
Background	6½
Fan Accent	1
First and Third Borders – pieced	1¼
Second Border – pieced	1⅝
Backing – 3 panels pieced crosswise	8¼
Binding – cut 2½" strips crosswise	⅞

Cutting Main Fabric A

Prepare the main fabric, following the directions on pages 12–17. Use Pattern F on page 127 to make a fan wedge template from paper or template plastic. Ordering information for an acrylic wedge ruler is included in the Sources section on page 135.

Stack-n-Whack Chart for Fan Quilt		
Cut layers 21" wide. Cut 6 identical layers for each stack. Use a different set of identical layers for each additional stack.		
If the lengthwise design repeat is:	Use this many design repeats for each layer:	Make this many stacks:
6"–10"	Three repeats	2
11"–17"	Two repeats	2
Over 17"	One repeat	2
Whack...	**To Make...**	
(4) 8¾" strips; whack (10) fan blade wedges from each strip	(32) fan blade wedge block kits	

To cut the fan wedges, place the wedge template at one end of the strip set, aligning the short sides with the strip edges, and cut along both long sides. If you are using a paper or thin plastic template, use a ruler as a straight edge to protect the template (Fig. 2–68).

Turn the template so the wider end is at the opposite edge of the strip set, aligning the cut edges, and cut to make the next block kit. Continue cutting wedges from the strip, turning the template each time (Fig. 2–69).

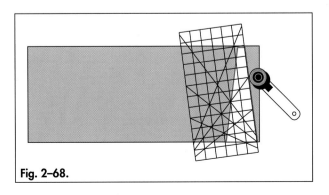

Fig. 2–68.

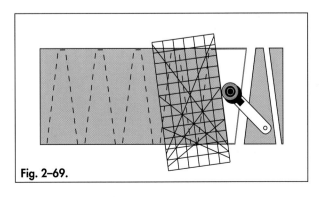

Fig. 2–69.

Cutting Background Fabric		
First Cut	**Second Cut**	**Third Cut**
(2) 18¼" strips across width	(4) 18¼" squares – 2 per strip	Cut each square twice on the diagonal to make (14) side triangles, plus two extras
(1) 9⅜" strip across width	(2) 9⅜" squares	Cut each square once on the diagonal to make (4) corner triangles
(6) 12½" strips across width for blocks	(18) 12½" squares – 3 per strip	
(2) 3½" x 92" lengthwise strips	Set aside for side setting strips	
(1) 6½" x 70" lengthwise strip	Set aside for bottom setting strip	
From the remaining width of fabric – approximately 28" – cut:		
(7) 12½" strips across the width for blocks	(14) 12½" squares – 2 per strip	

Cutting the Borders	
First and Third Borders	Cut (19) 2" strips across the width. Piece the strips together into one long strip.
Second Border	Cut (9) 5½" strips across the width. Piece the strips together into one long strip.

Preparing Accent Fabric Bias Strips

From Fan Accent Fabric, cut two 13" strips across the width. Working with the fabric unfolded, cut 1" bias strips from the 13" strips. You will need 32 strips approximately 16" long for the outer edges of the fans. Extra strips and the shorter strips from each side of the fabric can be used for the inner edges of the fans (Fig. 2–70).

Taking care not to stretch the bias edges, press each strip in half lengthwise so that it is ½" wide (Fig. 2–71).

Piecing the Fan Blocks

Piece 32 fans as follows:

Each set of 6 identical wedges is one block kit (Fig. 2–72).

With right sides together, piece a pair of wedges from one block kit (Fig. 2–73).

Open the pair of wedges (Fig. 2–74).

Repeat with two additional pairs. Piece the three pairs together. Press the seam allowances to one side (Fig. 2–75).

With raw edges aligned, apply the bias strip to the outer edge of the fan (Fig. 2–76).

Piecing the Fan Blocks

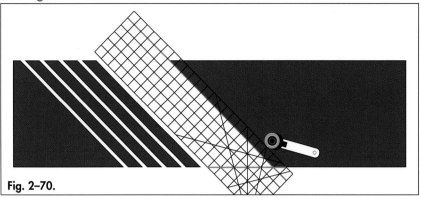

Fig. 2–70.

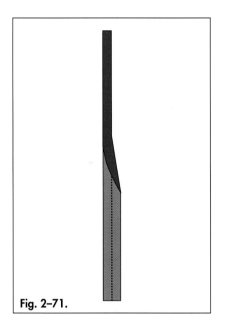

Fig. 2–71.

Fig. 2–72.

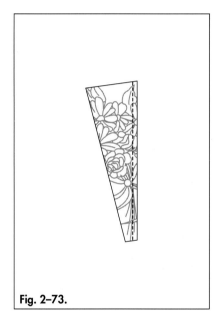

Fig. 2–73.

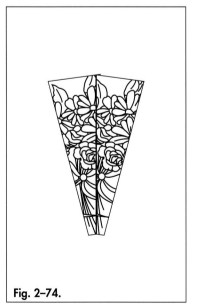

Fig. 2–74.

Fig. 2–75.

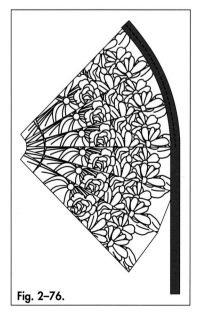

Fig. 2–76.

Turn the raw edges of the bias strip to the back of the fan and press lightly (Fig. 2–77).

With raw edges aligned, apply the bias strip to the inner edge of the fan. Work with the fan pieces on top, straightening the edge gently as you attach the strip (Fig. 2–78).

Clip the edge nearly to the seam line (Fig. 2–79).

Turn the raw edges to the back of the fan and press lightly (Fig. 2–80).

Lay the fan on a 12½" square of background fabric. Baste in place along the straight edges of the fan. Trim any extra length from the bias strips (Fig. 2–81).

Stitch the fan to the background square along the curved edges by sewing in the seam lines between the wedges and the bias trim (Fig. 2–82).

Assembling the Quilt

Arrange the fan blocks and setting triangles, following the quilt assembly diagram. Sew the seams in each diagonal row, then sew the diagonal rows together.

Measure across the width in the center of the quilt, and cut the 6½" x 70" strip of background fabric to this length. Sew this strip to the bottom of the quilt. Measure the quilt top down the center and cut the (2) 3½" x 92" strips to this length. Sew these strips to the long sides.

Cutting the Borders

The borders have butted corners. Measure the quilt top down the center and cut 2 narrow borders this length. Sew the borders to two opposite sides. Measure across the width in the center of the quilt, including borders, and cut 2

Piecing the Fan Blocks (cont.)

Fig. 2–77.

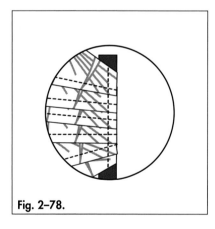

Fig. 2–78.

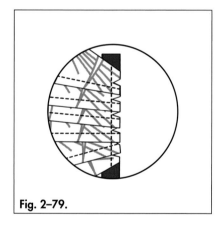

Fig. 2–79.

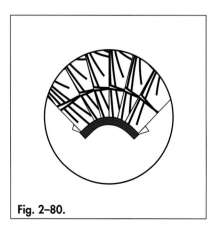

Fig. 2–80.

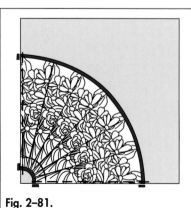

Fig. 2–81.

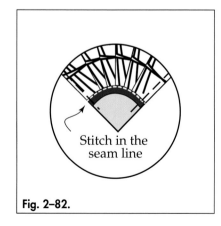

Stitch in the seam line

Fig. 2–82.

borders this length. Sew them to the top and bottom.

Repeat for the second and third border, using the remaining strip of narrow border fabric for the third border.

Finishing the Quilt

Prepare the backing by piecing together three 2¾-yard lengths of backing fabric. Layer the quilt top, batting, and backing. Quilt the layers and bind the raw edges.

Quilting Notes

Each fan is outline quilted. Two rows of quilting, stitched with a wide twin needle, accentuate the fan wedges in and alongside each seam line. All-over quilting fills the background and wide border.

Quilt assembly.

PART THREE:

Mirror-Image Magic

How the Magic Mirror-Image Trick Works

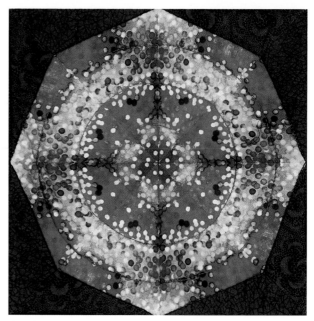

detail ROUNDABOUT STARS

U sing the Stack-n-Whack method results in designs with radial symmetry. This means that the designs rotate around the center of the block, much like blades on a windmill. Another type of symmetry is bilateral symmetry, in which portions of the design form mirror images on either side of an axis line. Quilt blocks with bilateral symmetry often appear to burst from the center. This is the type of symmetry you will see if you place a pair of mirrors on a fabric design, but it is usually not the type you will see in your finished quilt block unless you begin with a print that has a symmetrical design. You need to cut the pieces with careful attention to the placement of the axis line. The Stack-n-Select directions, beginning on page 72, detail this special process.

The Magic Mirror-Image Trick is an easy way to create a mirror-image effect without selective cutting. The secret lies in using both the front and back of the fabric.

To see how a print might be used with the Magic Mirror-Image Trick, fold the reverse side of the fabric back over the front side. Slide the edge over until you find the point where the pattern mirrors. You can fold the fabric on either the lengthwise or crosswise grain for this test (Plate 1).

The type of image you see along the mirror-image line approximates the effect you will have at the seam line between two pieces (Plates 2, 3, and 4).

Prints with light backgrounds tend to work best for this method, but don't rule out any print until you have looked at both sides. The two sides do not have to be identical to create the mirror-image effect. Slight variations will not be very noticeable in the finished block. When the two sides are quite different, a transparent or dimensional effect may appear, as on page 66 in KAREN'S TRANSPARENT STAR.

For the Magic Mirror-Image Trick, stack all the layers right side up. Cut the block kits from strips, as for the basic Stack-n-Whack method. No special placement is necessary. Any part of the design will produce a unique mirror-image (Plate 5).

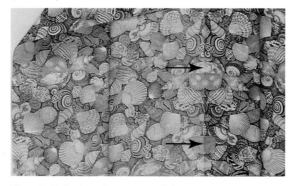

Plate 1. Slide the edge over until the pattern mirrors.

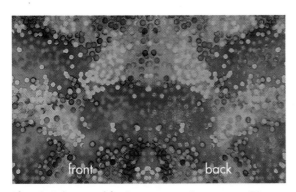

Plate 2. Fabric used for ROUNDABOUT STARS, page 59.

Plate 3. Fabric used for BUTTERFLIES, page 52.

Plate 4. Fabric used for KAREN'S STAR, page 66.

together. For mirror-image piecing, the right side of one patch is sewn to the reverse side of the adjacent patch. Some people find it helpful to lay out all the block pieces before sewing them together. If you choose to do this, be sure to note which pieces are reverse side up. You can use the finished block illustration as a guide in arranging the patches.

You can apply this method to many types of blocks. The fan block in Plate 8 is pieced in the traditional manner, while the one in Plate 9 is pieced with the Magic Mirror-Image method.

Plate 5. Mirror-image block kits can be cut from any part of the print.

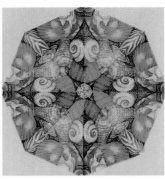

Plate 6. Regular Stack-n-Whack.   Plate 7. Mirror image.

When you piece the block, simply use the reverse side of every other piece as the right side. Plate 6 shows how the triangles look with all fabrics facing up. Plate 7 shows the same pieces with every other triangle turned over to produce the mirror-image effect.

The directions for projects in this chapter will guide you through the mirror-image process. The illustrations show the reverse side of the fabric in lighter shades. In conventional piecing, patches are sewn with right sides

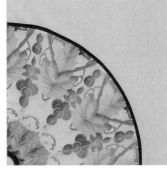

Plate 8. Regular Stack-n-Whack, made by Eleanor Carlisle.   Plate 9. Mirror-image, made by Eleanor Carlisle.

BUTTERFLIES

54" x 47", made by the author.

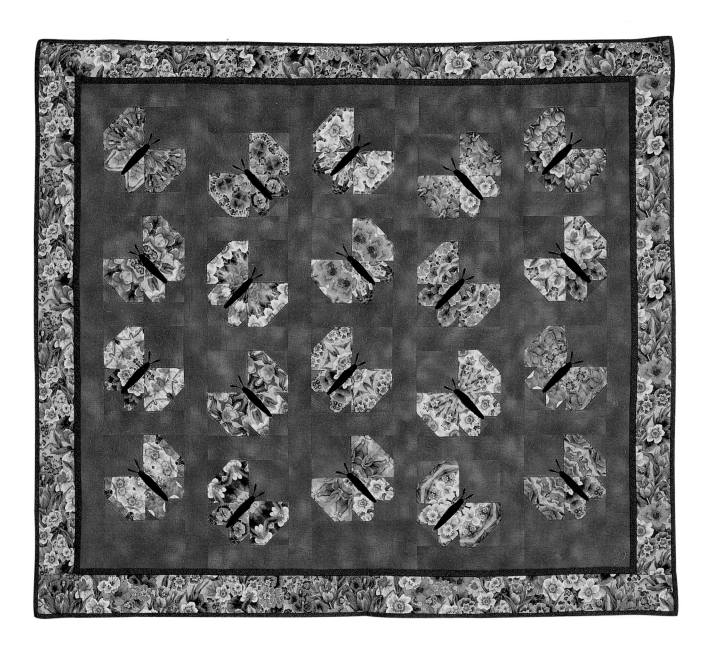

detail Butterflies

BUTTERFLIES

Finished Quilt Top: 54" x 47"
Finished Block: 7"

Intermediate

The Magic Mirror-Image Trick creates unique butterflies from a single print. Add machine or hand appliqué and a bit of embroidery, and you have a butterfly garden to envy! Read pages 50–51 before selecting your main fabric.

Fabric Requirements					
Measurements in yards unless otherwise indicated.					
If the design repeat of **Main Fabric A** is	6"–10"	11"–14"	15"–23"	23"–27"	over 27"
You will need this many yards	3¾	3½	5¾	6½	8 repeats

Additional Fabrics	
Background B	1¾
Butterfly Bodies	⅛
Inner Border – pieced	¼
Outer Border*	⅝ – cut crosswise or 1¾ – cut lengthwise
Backing – pieced lengthwise	3
Binding – cut 2½" strips crosswise	⅝

* The main fabric yardage includes the outer border. If you would like to use a different border fabric, this is the extra yardage you will need, but don't reduce the Main Fabric yardage.

Cutting Main Fabric A

Prepare the main fabric, following the directions on pages 12–17. See pages 110–111 for general instructions on cutting 45-degree triangles. Use the pattern on page 122 for the Butterfly body and check the block kits for accuracy by using the guide.

Stack-n-Whack Chart for Butterflies Quilt		
Cut layers 21" wide. Cut 8 identical layers for each stack. Use a different set of identical layers for each additional stack.		
If the lengthwise design repeat is:	Use this many design repeats for each layer:	Make this many stacks:
6"–11"	One repeat	2
Over 11"	One repeat	1
Whack...		**To Make...**
(2) 5" strips; whack 45° triangle wedges		(15) 45° triangle block kits (8 per strip) ▲

Cut each triangle wedge kit up the center to make the BUTTERFLY half-wedge block kits. Note that the triangles are either left-facing (bottom point faces left) or right-facing (bottom point faces right) (Figs. 3–1 and 3–2).

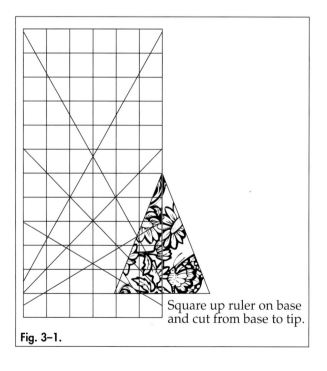

Square up ruler on base and cut from base to tip.

Fig. 3–1.

Left-facing Triangle   Right-facing Triangle

Fig. 3–2.

Cutting Background Fabric B – Blocks			
Position in Block	**First Cut**	**Second Cut**	**Third Cut**
B1	(3) 1½" strips across width	(80) 1½" squares	
B2	(3) 3" strips across width	(30) 3" squares	Cut each square once on the diagonal to make (60) half-square triangles
B3	(2) 4" strips across width	(20) 4" squares	

Cutting Background Fabric B – Sashing		
Position in Quilt	**First Cut**	**Second Cut**
Horizontal Sashing	(4) 2½" strips across width	(20) 2½" x 7½" rectangles
Horizontal Sashing	(1) 4½" strip across width	(5) 4½" x 7½" rectangles
Vertical Sashing	(6) 2½" strips across width	

Adding Borders	
Position	**Cut**
Inner Border	(5) 1" strips across width
Outer Border	(5) 3½" x 42" strips. For directional fabrics, cut 2 strips lengthwise and 3 strips across the width

Piecing the Butterfly Blocks

Piece 20 BUTTERFLY blocks as follows:

Each butterfly block is made from one set of 8 identical half-wedge triangles and one-half (four pieces) of a second set.

Choose a set of eight identical triangles for the upper wings. With the front of one triangle facing the back of the other triangle, sew the triangles together along their longest sides (Figs. 3–3 and 3–4, page 56).

Repeat with three more pairs. Finger-press the seam allowances open (Fig. 3–5, page 56).

Piece the pairs together into 2 sets of 4 for the upper wings. Press the seam allowances open (Figs. 3–6 and 3–7, page 56).

Choose a second set of right-facing triangles for the lower wings. Set aside 4 of the triangles for another block. Piece 2 pairs with the front of one triangle facing the back of the other triangle as shown (Figs. 3–8 and 3–9, page 56).

Add B1 squares to the right-angle corners of each lower-wing pair. Stitch diagonally across the squares as shown (Fig. 3–10, page 56).

Trim the seam allowances to ¼" (Fig. 3–11).

Piecing the Butterfly Blocks

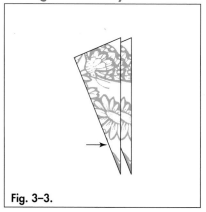

Fig. 3–3.

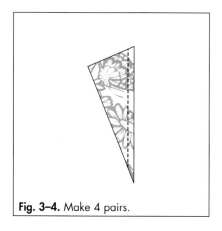

Fig. 3–4. Make 4 pairs.

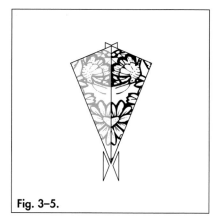

Fig. 3–5.

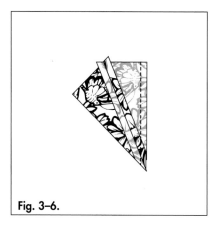

Fig. 3–6.

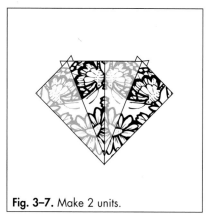

Fig. 3–7. Make 2 units.

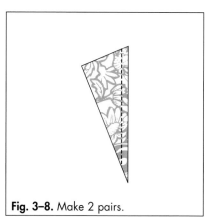

Fig. 3–8. Make 2 pairs.

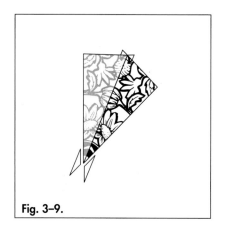

Fig. 3–9.

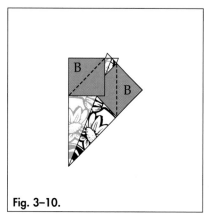

Fig. 3–10.

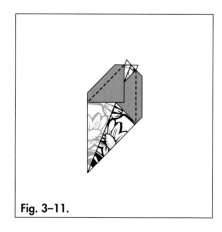

Fig. 3–11.

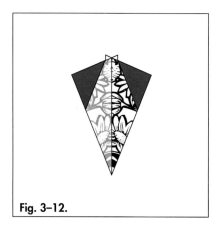

Fig. 3–12.

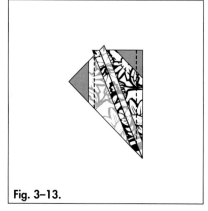

Fig. 3–13.

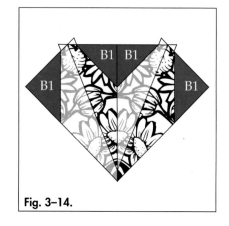

Fig. 3–14.

Piecing the Butterfly Blocks (cont.)

Finger-press, pushing the seam allowances toward the added triangles (Fig. 3–12).

Join the 2 pairs. Press the seam allowances open (Figs. 3–13 and 3–14).

Add a B2 triangle to the corner of each wing unit as shown. Press the seam allow-ances toward the triangles (Figs. 3–15, 3–16, 3–17, and 3–18).

Arrange the 3 wing units and a B3 square. Piece togeth-er, pushing the half-block seam allowances in opposite directions (Fig. 3–19).

Appliqué the butterfly bodies by machine or hand. For appliqué tips, see pages 116–117. Machine or hand embroider the antennae (Fig. 3–20).

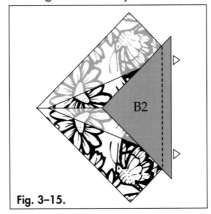

Fig. 3–15.

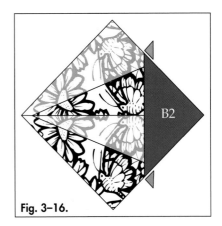

Fig. 3–16.

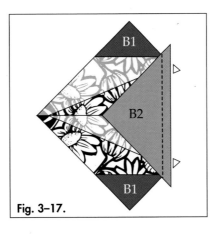

Fig. 3–17.

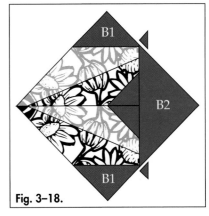

Fig. 3–18.

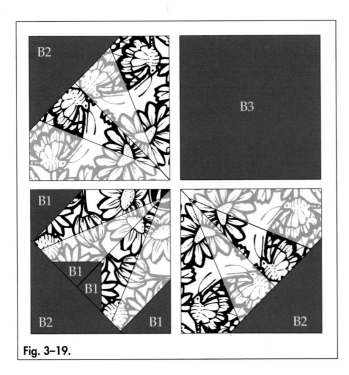

Fig. 3–19.

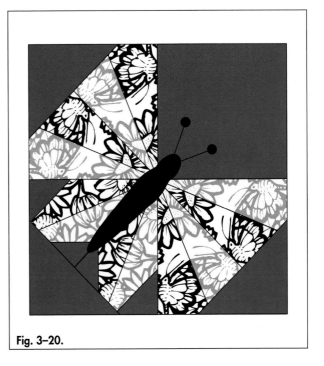

Fig. 3–20.

Arrange the blocks and sashing strips, following the quilt assembly diagram and turning the butterfly blocks as needed. Sew the horizontal sashing between the blocks in each vertical column. Sew the columns together, adding the long vertical sashing strips.

Adding the Borders

The borders have butted corners.

For the inner border, measure the quilt top down the center (the shorter dimension) and cut two border strips this length. Sew the borders to the sides. Piece three strips together into one long strip. Measure across the width in the center of the quilt, including borders, and cut two border strips this length. Sew them to the top and bottom.

For the outer border, measure the quilt top down the center (the shorter dimension) and cut 2 border strips this length. Sew the strips to the sides. (For directional fabrics, such as the one shown in the sample quilt, use 2 length-wise strips.) Piece together the 3 remaining strips. Measure across the width in the center of the quilt, including borders, and cut 2 border strips this length. Sew them to the top and bottom.

Finishing the Quilt

Prepare the backing by piecing together two 1⅜-yard lengths of backing fabric. Layer the quilt top, batting, and backing. Quilt the layers and bind the raw edges.

Quilting Notes

Free-motion quilting, about ¼" from the seams, outlines the butterflies in the background fabric. The upper wings have a heart-shaped quilting design, and the lower wings have teardrop loops. Quilting also outlines the appliquéd body and embroidered antennae. Meander quilting fills the background areas and outer border. The narrow border is quilted in the seam lines.

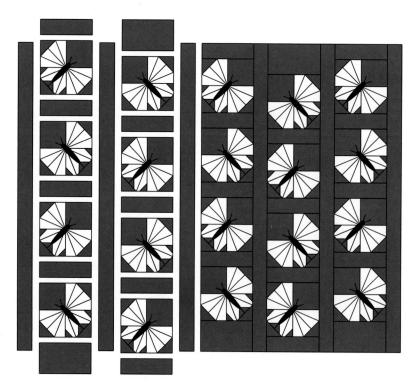

Quilt assembly.

ROUNDABOUT STARS
50" x 70", made by the author.

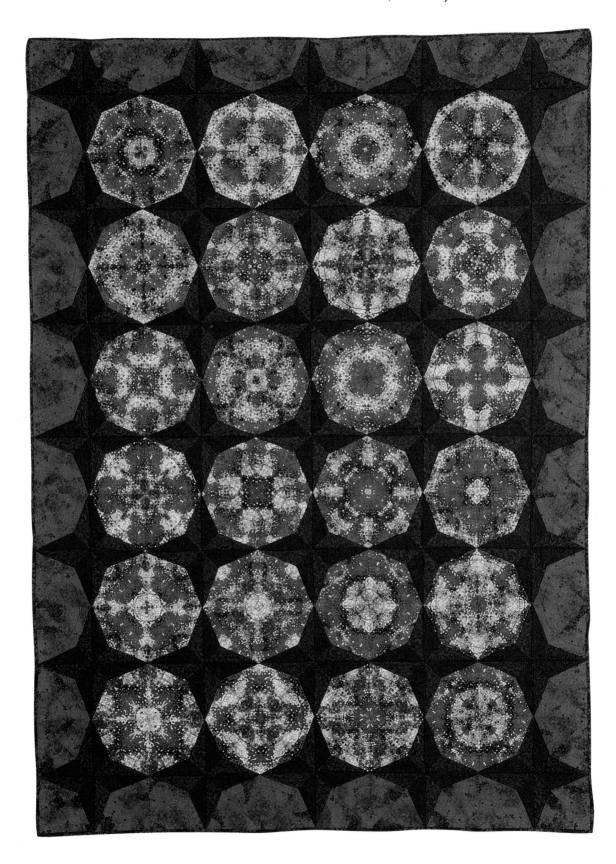

ROUNDABOUT STARS

Finished Quilt Top: 50" x 70"
Finished Block: 10"

Intermediate

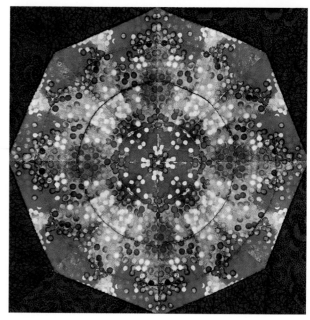

detail ROUNDABOUT STARS

T hanks to the Magic Mirror-Image Trick, the octagonal centers of these blocks explode in colorful symmetrical designs. Four-point stars form where the block corners meet. Read pages 50–51 before selecting your main fabric.

Fabric Requirements					
Measurements in yards unless otherwise indicated.					
If the design repeat of **Main Fabric A** is	6"–10"	11"–14"	15"–20"	21"–27"	over 27"
You will need this many yards	5	3½	5	6½	8 repeats
Additional Fabrics					
Star Points B and C	⅞ each				
Border D	1				
Backing	3¼				
Binding	⅝				

Cutting Main Fabric A

Prepare the main fabric, following the directions on pages 12–17. See pages 110–111 for general instructions on cutting 45-degree triangles. Check the block kits for accuracy by using the guides on page 126.

Stack-n-Whack Chart for Roundabout Stars Quilt		
Cut layers 21" wide. Cut 8 identical layers for each stack. Use a different set of identical layers for each additional stack.		
If the lengthwise design repeat is:	Use this many design repeats for each layer:	Make this many stacks:
6"–10"	Two repeats	2
11"–23"	One repeat	2
Over 23"	One repeat	1
Whack...		**To Make...**
(4) 5½" strips; whack 45° triangle wedges		(24) 45° triangle block kits (6 per strip) ▲

Cutting Star Fabrics B and C and Border Fabric D		
Fabric	First Cut	Second Cut
B and C	(14) 2" strips across width from each color	(140) triangles each of B and C*
D	(6) 5½" strips across width; whack 45° triangle wedges – 16 per strip	(88) 45° triangle wedges
*Follow the cutting instructions carefully. The B and C triangles are not alike.		

Cutting the Star Fabric Triangles

Layer a pair of 2" strips of colors B and C, wrong sides together. If you are right-handed, place Fabric C on top. If you are left-handed, place Fabric B on top (Fig. 3–21).

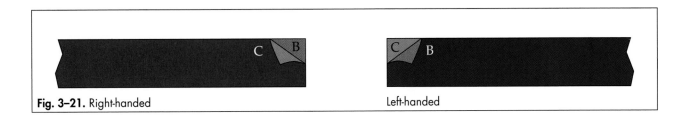

Fig. 3–21. Right-handed   Left-handed

Cutting the Star Fabric Triangles (cont.)

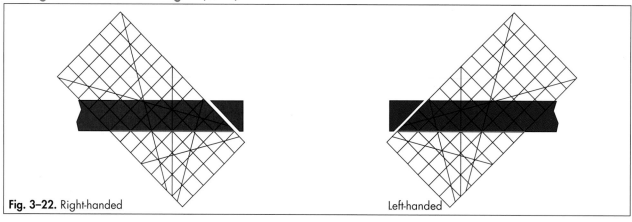

Fig. 3–22. Right-handed   Left-handed

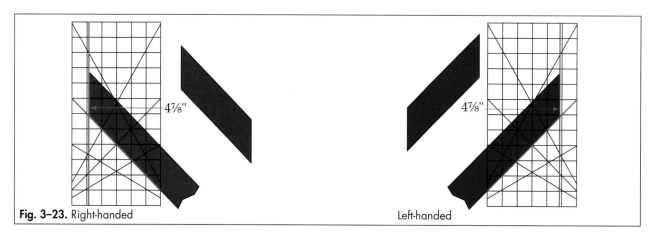

Fig. 3–23. Right-handed   Left-handed

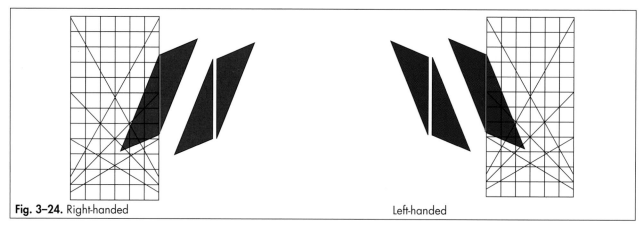

Fig. 3–24. Right-handed   Left-handed

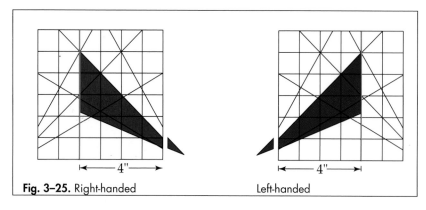

Fig. 3–25. Right-handed   Left-handed

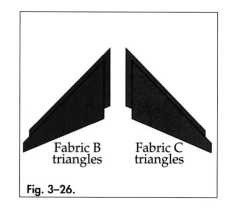

Fabric B triangles   Fabric C triangles

Fig. 3–26.

Trim one end of the strip set at a 45-degree angle as shown (Fig. 3–22).

Turn the strip set so that the angled edge is to your left if you are right handed or to your right if you are left-handed. Place the 4⅞" ruler line on the angled edge. The 45-degree line should be on one long edge. Cut to make the shape shown (Fig. 3–23).

To make triangle sets, keep the 2 colors layered and cut the shapes from corner to corner as shown (Figs. 3–24).

Place the 4" line of the ruler on the short side of each triangle set and trim off the skinny tip (Figs. 3–25).

Whether you are cutting left- or right-handed, you should now have four triangles. The triangles of Fabric B and Fabric C should be reversed in shape (Fig. 3–26).

To check the accuracy of these pieces, use the guides on page 127.

Piecing Roundabout Star Blocks

Piece 24 Roundabout Star blocks as follows:

Each set of 8 identical wedges is 1 block kit.

Add Fabric B triangles to 4 identical wedges, as follows: Place the front side of Fabric B against the reverse side of the Main Fabric. Align the triangle with the shortest side of the wedge. The blunted tip of the B triangle should align with the adjacent side, and the pointed end of the B triangle should extend beyond the wedge as shown (Fig. 3–27).

Finger-press the seam allowances toward the B triangle (Fig. 3–28).

Add Fabric C triangles to the other 4 wedges. The 2 fabrics should be right sides together this time. The pointed end of the C triangle will extend beyond the wedge as shown (Fig. 3–29).

Finger-press the seam allowances toward the C triangle (Fig. 3–30).

Piecing the Roundabout Star Blocks

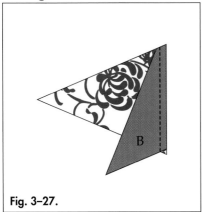

Fig. 3–27.

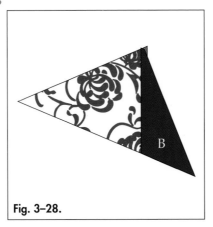

Fig. 3–28.

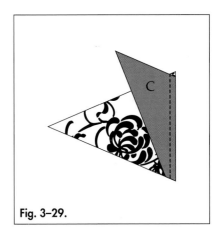

Fig. 3–29.

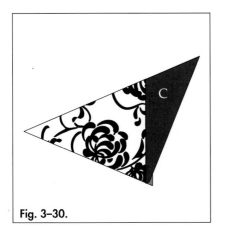

Fig. 3–30.

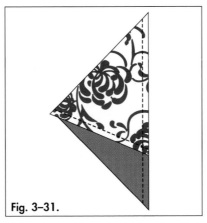

Fig. 3–31.

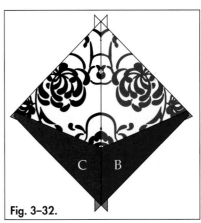

Fig. 3–32.

Sew the A/B and the A/C units together in pairs to make quarter-blocks (Fig. 3–31, page 63).

Press the seam allowances open. If you use an iron, take care to avoid the off-grain edges of the wedges (Fig. 3–32, page 63).

Sew the quarter-blocks together to make half-blocks. Press the seam allowances open (Fig. 3–33).

Sew the half-blocks together to complete the block. Press the seam allowances open (Figs. 3–34 and 3–35).

Piecing the Roundabout Star Blocks (cont.)

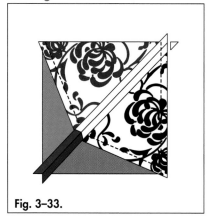

Fig. 3–33.

Fig. 3–34.

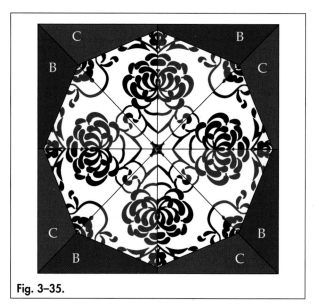

Fig. 3–35.

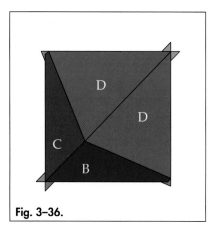

Fig. 3–36.

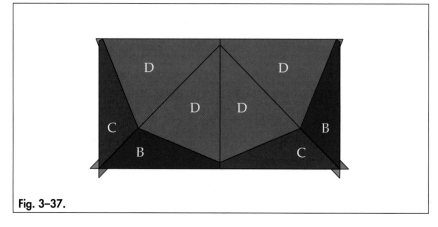

Fig. 3–37.

Piecing the Border and Corner Blocks

Piece 44 quarter-blocks, substituting border fabric D for Main Fabric A and placing all pieces right sides together (Fig. 3–36).

Piece together 20 pairs of quarter-blocks to make 20 half-blocks (Fig. 3–37). The remaining 4 units are the corner blocks.

Assembling the Quilt

Arrange the quilt blocks, following the quilt assembly diagram. Sew the vertical seams in each row, then sew the horizontal rows together.

Finishing the Quilt

Prepare the backing by piecing together two 1⅝-yard lengths of backing fabric. Layer the quilt top, batting, and backing. Quilt the layers and bind the raw edges.

Quilting Notes

The stars are quilted on the seam lines. Concentric circles are quilted in each block center. The circles are 2½", 5", and 7½" in diameter. Half-circles with the same spacing are quilted in the border blocks.

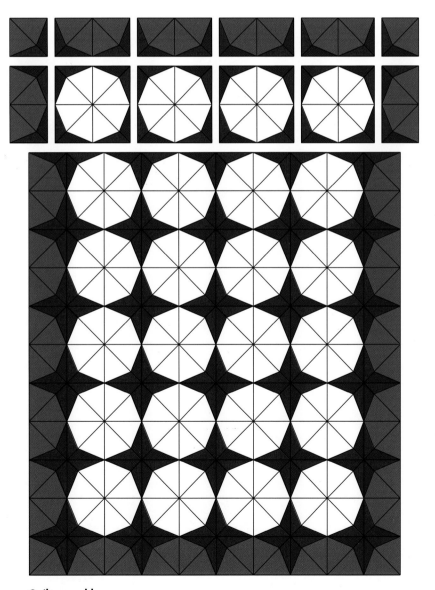

Quilt assembly.

KAREN'S TRANSPARENT STAR

66" x 90", made by the author. Quilt designed by Karen Combs.

detail KAREN'S TRANSPARENT STAR

KAREN'S TRANSPARENT STAR

Finished Quilt Top: 66" x 90"
Finished Block: 12"

Easy

Karen Combs' magic touch with color and illusion is apparent in these overlapping stars. To achieve the transparent effect, Karen recommends choosing two colors of the same intensity. The two light shades (in this quilt, the light teal and light rose) should be close in value, and the two darker shades (here, the dark teal and dark rose) should also be close in value.

The Magic Mirror-Image Trick produces differences in the color intensity of the main fabric to create another suggestion of transparency. Read pages 50–51 for more about this method before selecting your main fabric.

Fabric Requirements					
Measurements in yards unless otherwise indicated.					
If the design repeat of **Main Fabric A** is	6"–10"	11"–14"	15"–20"	21"–27"	over 27"
You will need this many yards	5	6½	5	6½	8 repeats

Additional Fabrics	
B – lighter shade, color 1 – light teal in sample	1⅝
C – darker shade, color 1 – dark teal in sample	1
D – lighter shade, color 2 – light rose in sample	1½
E – darker shade, color 2 – dark rose in sample	1
Backing – pieced lengthwise	5½
Binding – cut 2½" strips crosswise	¾

Cutting Main Fabric A

Prepare the main fabric, following the directions on pages 12–17. See page 108 for general instructions on cutting half-square triangles. Check block kits for accuracy by using the guide on page 127.

Stack-n-Whack Chart for Karen's Transparent Star Quilt		
Cut layers 21" wide. Cut 8 identical layers for each stack. Use a different set of identical layers for each additional stack.		
If the lengthwise design repeat is:	Use this many design repeats for each layer:	Make this many stacks:
6"–16"	Two repeats	2
Over 16"	One repeat	2
Whack...		**To Make...**
(7) 3⅞" strips; whack 5 squares from each strip and cut each square once on the diagonal		(70) half-square triangle block kits (10 per strip)

Cutting Accent Fabric Triangles			
Fabric	First Cut	Second Cut	Third Cut
B	(13) 3⅞" strips across width	(122) 3⅞" squares – 10 per strip	Cut each square once on the diagonal to make (244) triangles
C	(5) 3⅞" strips across width	(50) 3⅞" squares – 10 per strip	Cut each square once on the diagonal to make (100) triangles
D	(12) 3⅞" strips across width	(112) 3⅞" squares – 10 per strip	Cut each square once on the diagonal to make (224) triangles
E	(5) 3⅞" strips across width	(44) 3⅞" squares – 10 per strip	Cut each square once on the diagonal to make (88) triangles

Cutting Accent Fabric Squares for Border Blocks		
Fabric	First Cut	Second Cut
C	(3) 3½" strips across width	(32) 3½" squares – 12 per strip
E	(2) 3½" strips across width	(20) 3½" squares – 12 per strip

Piecing the Block Centers

For each block center, you will need one block kit (8 identical triangles).

Sew 4 pairs of triangles, placing both triangles right side up rather than right sides together (Figs. 3–38 and 3–39). Press the seam allowances to one side (Fig. 3–40).

Arrange the 4 squares as shown, so that the triangles that are right side up form a pinwheel that spins clockwise. Piece 35 block centers (Fig. 3–41).

B/C Blocks (teal)

Make 100 squares from the B and C triangles, placing the fabrics right sides together (Fig. 3–42).

Count out 18 of the remaining block kits.

Working on one block at a time, sew the main fabric triangles to B triangles, as follows: For four pairs, lay the main fabric triangle on top, with both pieces right side up (Fig. 3–43).

Sew the long bias edges together (Fig. 3–44).

Press the seam allowances toward the main fabric triangle (Fig. 3–45).

On the remaining 4 pairs, place the B triangle and main fabric triangle right sides together (Fig. 3–46).

Sew the bias edges together (Fig. 3–47).

Press the seam allowances toward the main fabric triangle (Fig. 3–48).

Piecing the Blocks

Fig. 3–38.

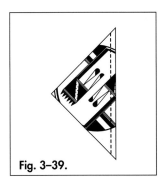

Fig. 3–39.

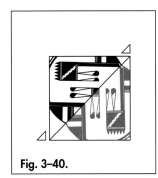

Fig. 3–40.

Fig. 3–41.

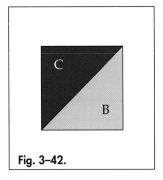

Fig. 3–42.

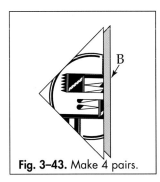

Fig. 3–43. Make 4 pairs.

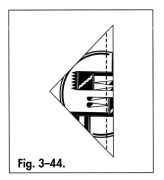

Fig. 3–44.

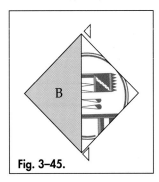

Fig. 3–45.

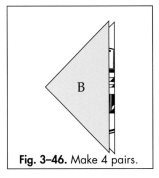

Fig. 3–46. Make 4 pairs.

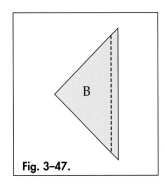

Fig. 3–47.

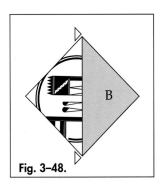

Fig. 3–48.

Arrange the squares as shown, with the right-side-up triangle on the right (Fig. 3–49).

Flip the right square over onto the left square and sew together (Fig. 3–50).

Press the seam allowances to one side. Make 4 of these A/B units for each block (Fig. 3–51).

Sew a B/C pieced square to each end of 2 A/B units for each block. Press the seam allowances toward the B/C squares. Do not sew squares to the remaining 2 units. Keep the 4 units for the block together (Fig. 3–52).

Place the A/B units as shown and preview the various block centers (Fig. 3–53).

When you have found an interesting combination, sew the two A/B units to the center square. Press the seam allowances toward the center. Add the top and bottom A/B/C units. Press the seam allowances away from the center (Fig. 3–54).

D/E Blocks (rose)

Use 17 block kits for the D/E blocks.

Make 88 squares from the D and E triangles, placing the fabrics right sides together.

Piece in the same manner as for the B/C blocks, substituting D for B and E for C (Fig. 3–55).

Piecing the Blocks (cont.)

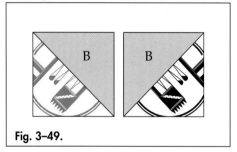

Fig. 3–49.

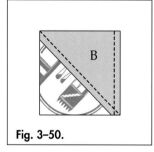

Fig. 3–50.

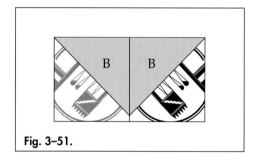

Fig. 3–51.

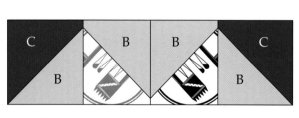

Fig. 3–52.

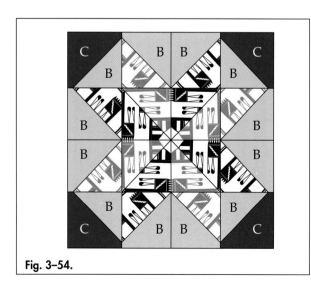

Fig. 3–54.

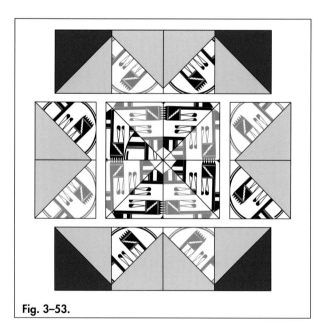

Fig. 3–53.

Border Units

Make 14 pairs of B/C squares and 10 pairs of D/E squares. Press the seam allowances to one side.

Piece the border units as shown, combining them with unpieced squares of C and E. Press the seam allowances toward the squares (Figs. 3–56 and 3–57).

Assembling the Quilt

Arrange the blocks and border units according to the quilt assembly diagram. Place squares of Fabric C in the corners. Sew the blocks together in rows. Sew the rows together to complete the top.

Finishing the Quilt

Prepare the backing by cutting the yardage in half and sewing the pieces together lengthwise. Layer the quilt top, batting, and backing. Quilt the layers and bind the raw edges.

Quilting Notes

KAREN'S TRANSPARENT STAR is quilted in the seam lines along the straight sides of the star points, creating a square grid, and then along the bias seam lines and through the centers of the star blocks to create a diagonal grid. The background and accent fabrics are stipple quilted in variegated rayon threads to blend with the fabrics. In each block center, the four corners formed by the diagonal grid quilting are also stipple quilted. Free-motion quilting enhances the individual designs in the center of each block. The photo on page 67 shows a detail of the block quilting.

Piecing the Blocks (cont.)

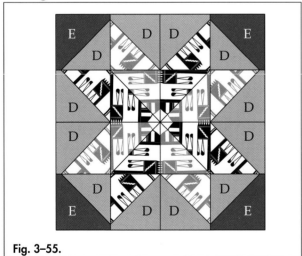

Fig. 3–55.

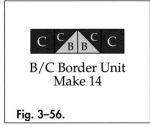

B/C Border Unit
Make 14

Fig. 3–56.

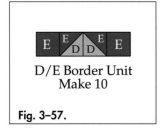

D/E Border Unit
Make 10

Fig. 3–57.

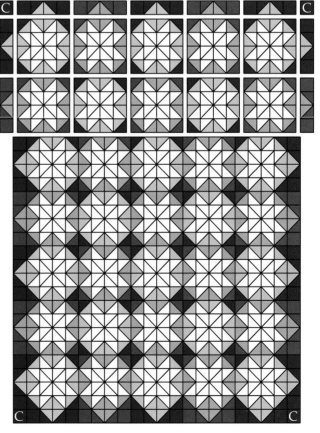

Quilt assembly.

PART FOUR:
Stack-n-Select

detail ARGYLE DIAMONDS

Watching designs magically appear without any pre-planning is part of the fun of Stack-n-Whack. Sometimes, though, a special fabric or quilt design will benefit from more controlled cutting. This does not mean you will need to individually cut each patch. By stacking identical layers and cutting selected areas, you can control the placement of fabric motifs without sacrificing time or accuracy.

This section includes projects especially suited to novelty prints and other projects designed especially for border and symmetrical prints. However, any Stack-n-Whack design can be selectively cut to control the placement of print motifs.

Methods for Selective Cutting & Stencil
Paper-Template Method

This simple, inexpensive method will work for any shape.

Cut templates of the shape needed from lightweight paper. Crisp, semi-transparent paper, such as vellum, works especially well. Include the seam allowance on the template. If the pattern calls for strip cutting, you can cut strips from the paper to quickly and accurately rotary cut the templates. If you need an odd shape, trace the shape first, then cut it with a rotary cutter and acrylic ruler. Although the templates can be re-used several times, cutting one template for each block kit needed will allow you to plan all the block kits before cutting them.

To aid in selecting the fabric area you want to use for your block kits, you can make a placement stencil. Trace the template on another piece of vellum, including the ¼" seam allowance. For symmetrical designs, draw a center line that extends into the seam allowance. Cut out the center of the new tracing on the seam line, leaving a template-shaped frame.

Cut and stack the layers as for random Stack-n-Whack cutting. Stick-pin the layers around all four sides, close to the edge.

Spray the back of the placement stencil and each template with temporary basting spray or use a bit of repositionable glue stick around the edges. Use the stencil to determine the placement of the templates on the stack, then slide the paper template underneath the stencil (Plate 1).

In placing the templates, try to keep a straight grain line on at least one edge of the piece to make piecing easier. Arrange as many pieces on the stack as possible before cutting, so that you can adjust the placement if desired.

If you are making more than one stack from the same fabric, arrange the templates on both stacks before cutting.

To rotary cut the block kits, place your acrylic ruler on each straight edge of the template to cut accurately and to protect the template (Plate 2).

Cut the block kits closest to the edges of the stack first. Trim away the odd scraps of fabric and pin around the templates in the center of the stack. Cut the remaining block kits.

If you prefer, you can use clear template plastic, replacing both the paper template and placement stencil. To make a clear template more visible on the fabric, outline the edge with a permanent marker in a color that contrasts with the fabric. You can also use plastic-coated freezer paper for the templates. Trace the templates on the uncoated side of the paper. Use a warm iron to temporarily adhere the freezer paper templates in place before cutting.

Acrylic-Template Method

Acrylic templates have some advantages over paper templates. They are accurate and easy to cut around and because they are transparent, placement is simple. There are many pre-cut acrylic templates available for quilters. You can also make your own or have them cut for you by a local business, such as a glass replacement shop. See page 135 for some mail-order sources for pre-made and custom-made acrylic templates.

For fabrics in which the design placement is more critical, such as symmetrical prints, mark the seam lines and center line on the template with a permanent or wet-erase marker.

Cut and stack the layers as for random Stack-n-Whack cutting. Stick-pin the layers around all four sides, close to the edge.

As you locate areas of the fabric that you would like to use for block kits, trace around the acrylic template with chalk, water-soluble pen, or other temporary marker. By tracing the

templates before cutting, you can plan the kits more carefully and rearrange as necessary (Plate 3).

Cut the block kits, placing the template on each traced outline as you cut. Cut the block kits closest to the edges of the stack first. If you have kits placed close together, be careful not to cut into adjacent kits. Trim away the odd scraps of fabric and pin around the kits in the center of the stack. Cut the remaining block kits.

Plate 1. Make a placement stencil for paper templates.

Plate 2. Use a ruler to protect paper templates when cutting.

Plate 3. Trace around acrylic templates to plan your cutting.

Determining Yardage for Stack-n-Select

Selective cutting requires more fabric than random cutting. Because patches usually will not fit together neatly like a jigsaw puzzle, a stack will yield fewer block kits. Estimating yardages for this approach depends on motif size and placement and on the creative decisions you make when selecting the cutting areas.

The quilt plans in this section of the book contain estimates for selective cutting. Here are some considerations in determining yardage for other designs.

- Most of the designs in this book can easily be adapted to fewer blocks. If you do not need a quilt of a particular size, you can simply play with the yardage you have and adjust the quilt design accordingly.

- If you want to make the number of blocks given in the project directions, allow for twice as many stacks when selectively cutting.

- If the Stack-n-Whack chart for a project calls for one stack in a particular repeat length, it will be possible to make a second stack from the other half of the width without adding to the yardage requirements. If the chart calls for two stacks, you will need additional yardage so that you can make three or four stacks.

- To determine the amount of yardage for additional stacks, use this formula:

Multiply the design repeat length (rounded to the nearest inch) by the number of design repeats in each layer by the number of layers in the stack. Divide the total by 36" to convert to yards.

Example:
Design repeat = 12"
Number of repeats in each layer = 2
Number of layers in each stack = 6
12 x 2 x 6 = 144"
144/36 = 4 yds.

- If you are using more than one main fabric, you can use the formula to determine the yardage needed for each print. Remember that the yardage requirements will vary depending on the design repeat length of each fabric. Fabrics with very long design repeats will require more yardage, but these prints often have more placement possibilities.

Plate 4. A print with distinct motifs on a plain ground.

Plate 5. Use Stack-n-Select to isolate motifs from a densely packed print.

Plate 6. Plan carefully to make the best use of separated motifs like this.

Novelty Prints

When working with novelty prints, study the fabric before purchasing or cutting it. Note the number of distinct motifs. Medium-scale novelty prints typically have 6–18 different motifs. They may be distinct, as in the alien-print fabric (Plate 4), or densely packed like the jungle fabric (Plate 5). Scenic prints, such as the penguin print in Plate 2 (page 73), tend to offer more placement options than prints with separated motifs.

If you want to feature a different motif in each block, you can select a print that has at least as many motifs as the number of blocks in the quilt or choose two or more compatible prints. Here is another trick to get more variety from a novelty fabric. If you feature the same motif a second time, rotate the template a quarter- or half-turn. This will change the overall pattern in the finished block.

Border Prints and Symmetrical Prints

You can add extra impact to quilt blocks by selectively cutting floral stripes, border prints, or symmetrical prints. To use these fabrics effectively, first study the print to see what design possibilities it contains.

There are several basic types of prints in this category, and each has characteristics that can enhance a design if used skillfully.

Take care when determining yardage for border stripes. First, determine the full-screen repeat length by finding the manufacturer's name on the selvage and measuring to the next repeat of the name (Plate 7).

It's important to find the full-screen repeat because the motifs in one band of the stripe may repeat three times per screen, while the motifs in the other bands may repeat two or four times. The French Provincial stripe in Plate 8 is a good example. The red lines across

the fabric show the true repeat. At the blue lines, the large grape leaves and the patterns in the blue stripes repeat, but the plums in the yellow stripe do not coincide.

If you are in doubt about the true repeat length, it is safest to use the screen repeat length as the design repeat length. If you use a full-screen repeat for each layer of the stack, the motifs should match up correctly in each layer, and you will also get maximum cutting versatility from the stack.

Stripes Without Symmetrical Elements

Simple lengthwise stripes with no noticeable lengthwise repeat, such as the ones in Plate 9, will not create very interesting Stack-n-Whack blocks. However, they can be effective as accent fabrics or borders.

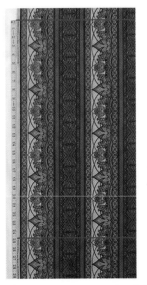 

Plate 7. Measure the full screen repeat.

Plate 8. Different bands of a stripe may have different repeat lengths.

Plate 9. Simple stripes like these do not work well for the main fabric.

Stripes that combine bands of different design elements offer possibilities for the Stack-n-Select method. In Medallion Star (page 91), you can see how floral stripe (Plate 10) can produce a medallion effect.

To create the medallion effect in a quilt block, place the side of the template that will be on the outer edges of the block parallel to the stripe (Plate 11).

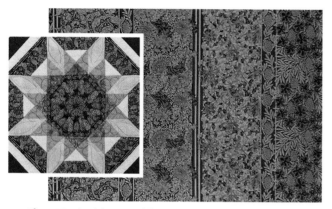

Plate 10. The fabric used for MEDALLION STAR (page 91).

Plate 11. Cutting for medallion effects.

Stripes With Symmetrical Elements

When a fabric contains symmetrical elements, you can use the Stack-n-Select method to produce blocks with bilateral, or mirror-image, symmetry. If the pieces are cut symmetrically, the printed motif will mirror along the center line of each piece. The design will also mirror along the seam lines between two identical pieces, creating a new symmetrical pattern and adding richness to the block. Compare the Stack-n-Whack blocks, which were cut from the same symmetrical print (Plates 12–14). The block on the left is cut randomly and seems to spin around the center point. The center block is cut selectively by the Stack-n-Select method. The design appears to radiate, and the same pattern appears at each seam line. The block on the right is cut with the Magic Mirror-Image Trick, described on page 50. This design also has bilateral symmetry, but different patterns appear at alternate seam lines.

If you have a print with symmetrical elements, study it to find the axis lines. An axis line is usually not an actual printed line, but rather an invisible line on each side of which the design mirrors or "flips." On the following pages, red lines such as those shown in Plate 15 indicate the axis lines.

To take advantage of mirror symmetry in a quilt block, you will need to place the center line of the cutting template on an axis line. A

Plate 12. Basic Stack-n-Whack.

Plate 13. Stack-n-Select.

Plate 14. Magic Mirror-Image.

motif may mirror for a very short distance or for many inches. Axis lines on border stripes typically run crosswise in the wider decorative bands and lengthwise in the narrower bands, but there are many variations.

You can move the template up and down this axis line for a certain distance to create different block designs. The number of different designs possible from a print will depend on the size of the template, the variety of axis lines, and the length between axis lines. In the photo of the brown stripe, notice that the smaller triangle fits within one band of the stripe. Pieces cut there would produce a symmetrical block. The larger triangle extends beyond the width of the band into adjacent bands. Because the motifs along the bottom of the triangle are not symmetrical (compare the fabric design at the points), pieces cut there would not produce a completely symmetrical block (Plate 16).

Even if only part of the design forms a symmetrical pattern, selective cutting can still add a special touch. In the print used for the fan blocks, only the large motif in the white-ground band has an axis line (Plates 17, 18, and 19).

As a rule, prints with longer lengthwise repeats will produce a greater variety of blocks. Prints with shorter repeats and fewer motifs, such as the pink stripe shown on the next page may be more efficient for cutting a number of identical blocks (Plate 20, page 78).

Plate 16. The larger triangle would not create a symmetrical block because the corners aren't identical

Plate 17.

Plate 18.

Plate 19.

Plates 17–19. The fan wedges were cut selectively to take advantage of the large symmetrical motif.

Plate 15. The red lines show the axis lines of the print.

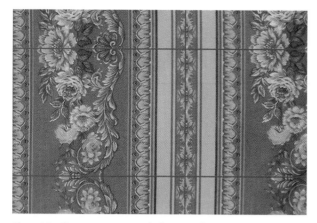

Plate 20. Shorter repeats with few motifs work best for identical blocks.

Plate 21. Checking printing accuracy with a ruler.

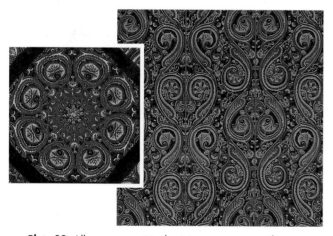

Plate 22. All-over symmetrical prints are very versatile.

Plate 23. An ogee print with axis lines in both directions.

The accuracy of the printed fabric is a concern when working with border prints and symmetrical prints. Printing on fabric is not like printing on metal or paper. Even high-quality fabrics may have some distortion or skewing across the width. A slight distortion will not affect the finished quilt block, but if a print has a great deal of skew, the cutting process can be frustrating, and the results disappointing. Before you use a fabric for mirror-symmetry effects, use a wide rotary cutting ruler to check that the lengthwise and cross-wise axis lines are perpendicular to each other. You can also fold the fabric across the width, matching lengthwise stripes, to see if the vertical designs fall into place correctly. If they are noticeably off, and if having less-than-perfect blocks will make you unhappy, look for another print or a more forgiving design (Plate 21).

All-over Symmetrical Prints

Not all symmetrical prints contain linear stripes. All-over symmetrical prints are harder to find, but offer wonderful possibilities for Stack-n-Select. As with border prints, the axis lines may run in one or both directions. But because the axis lines are not interrupted by striped bands, they are often longer and provide more opportunities for cutting different blocks.

The print used in VENETIAN TILES (page 100) is an example of an all-over print with lengthwise axis lines (Plate 22).

This print in Plate 23 is an example of an ogee print, a design based on oval shapes. It has uninterrupted axis lines running in both directions, making it especially versatile.

Plate 24 shows an interesting print with axis lines in both directions. The lengthwise axis lines are uninterrupted. Some are close together, so wider pieces might not fit within the symmetrical area. There are also shorter crosswise axis lines. A complex print like this one presents challenges but also intriguing possibilities.

As with border stripes, place the center line of the template on an axis line to produce mirror-image symmetry. The previous comments about print accuracy apply to these prints as well.

Partially Symmetrical Prints

Some fabrics contain symmetrical elements but are not truly symmetrical. In the multicolored geometric print, the colored rectangles form a symmetrical design with a number of axis lines, but the shaded corners in each rectangle mirror only along a single axis line down the center of the fabric width. For SECRET STAIRWAYS, about half the block kits were selectively cut to produce the bursting effect of bilateral symmetry, and the remaining blocks were randomly cut to produce the spinning effect of radial symmetry (Plate 25).

Another type of print is an all-over floral or scroll design in which the symmetry is somewhat loosely drawn. These prints create an impression of symmetry but contain some asymmetrical elements. If you are not concerned with absolute symmetry in the finished block, prints of this type can be attractive (Plate 26).

Piecing Blocks with Bilateral Symmetry

After you have carefully cut your block kits to produce these special effects, you will want to piece with equal care to achieve the best results. When you place two symmetrical pieces right sides together, the motifs should match. You can often correct minor discrepancies by aligning the motifs rather than the edges of the fabric. Pinning through the motifs in the center of two triangles to align them may help. Use the "stick-pinning" method described on page 16 for greater accuracy.

When piecing, you can "fudge" the seam allowances a little if necessary, by taking a slightly larger seam allowance on one piece or the other.

Press the finished block with steam and sizing to coax it into shape if needed. If you find the cut pieces are too far off for this kind of corrective surgery, the problem may lie with the accuracy of the print or with the stack pinning and cutting. In that case, this motto is offered up as food for thought:

IT DOESN'T HAVE TO BE PERFECT TO BE BEAUTIFUL.

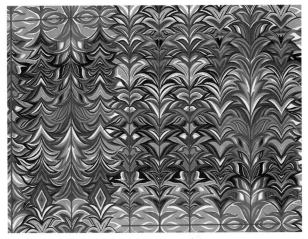

Plate 24. A print with unusual axis lines.

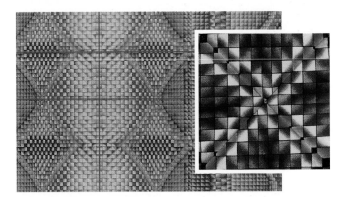

Plate 25. This print is partially symmetrical.

Plate 26. Some prints are not as symmetrical as they appear.

Novelty Windows

41" x 52", made by the author.

detail NOVELTY WINDOWS

NOVELTY WINDOWS

Finished Quilt Top: 41" x 52"
Finished Block: 10"

Easy

This nostalgic quilt contains motifs from two children's prints. Cut a placement stencil as described on pages 72–73 and use it to help find suitable choices for your windows. To enhance the illusion of depth, choose two shades of a single color for the window frames.

Fabric Requirements	
Measurements in yards unless otherwise indicated.	
Main Fabric A	4 or 8 design repeats each of two or more fabrics*
Additional Fabrics	
Side Window Frame B	⅜
Bottom Window Frame C	⅜
Sashing D	⅝
Narrow Accent Border	¼
Outer Border	⅝ – pieced or 1½ – seamless
Backing – pieced crosswise	2¾
Binding – cut 2½" strips crosswise	½
*For fabrics with shorter repeats, using two repeats in each layer will provide more placement options.	

Cutting Main Fabric A

Review the directions for selective cutting on pages 72–73. Use template W (page 128) for this design.

Stack-n-Select Chart for Novelty Windows Quilt		
Cut layers 21" wide. Cut 4 identical layers for each stack. Use a different set of identical layers for each additional stack.		
If the lengthwise design repeat is:	Use this many design repeats for each layer:	Make this many stacks:
6" and up	One repeat, or two repeats. Two repeats will provide better placement options on shorter repeats.	1 or 2 as needed
Selectively Whack...		
(12) right triangle block kits from two or more stacks using template W, centering a novelty print motif in each triangle		

Cutting Fabrics B, C, and D		
Fabric	First Cut	Second Cut
Side Window Frame B	(1) 11" strip across width	(12) 2½" x 11" rectangles
Bottom Window Frame C	(1) 11" strip across width	(12) 2½" x 11" rectangles
Vertical Sashing D	(1) 10½" strip across width	(16) 1½" x 10½" rectangles
Horizontal Sashing D	(5) 1½" x 36" strips across width	

Piecing the Novelty Windows Blocks

Piece 12 Novelty Windows blocks as follows:

Each set of 4 identical triangles is a block kit (Fig. 4–1).

Place 2 triangles from one block kit right sides together. Piece together on a short side. Repeat with the second pair of triangles. This is one set (Fig. 4–2).

Piece the block kits into sets of pairs. You can chain piece these. Clip the chain between each set of pairs to keep the matching pairs together (Fig. 4–3).

Place 2 matching pairs together, matching the seams at the center, and finger-press the seam allowances in opposite directions. Stitch part way down, stopping about 2" from the bottom tips (Fig. 4–4).

With the pieced square wrong side up, place a rectangle of Fabric B, right side up, under the right edge, as shown, and sew the pieces together. Finger-press the seam allowances toward the main fabric square (Fig. 4–5).

Turn the square right side up. Sew a rectangle of Fabric C to the right edge, right sides together. Finger-press the seam allowances toward the Fabric C rectangle (Figs. 4–6, and 4–7).

Fold the triangles with the seams and the straight edges aligned as shown. Trim the excess fabric from B and C to create a straight line along the bias edges. To do this accurately, align the edge of the ruler along the edge with the partial seam, and the 45-degree line of the ruler on the edge of the rectangular strip, as shown in Figure 4–8. Complete the partial seam (Fig. 4–9, page 84).

Press the seam allowances to one side. Trim the triangle tips to complete the block (Fig. 4–10, page 84).

Piecing the Novelty Windows Blocks

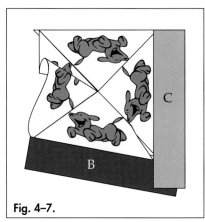

Fig. 4–1.

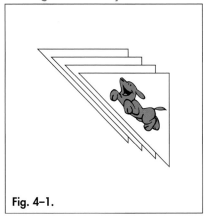

Fig. 4–2.

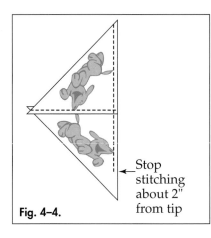

Fig. 4–3.

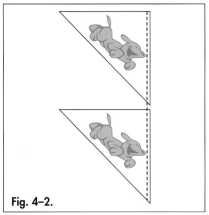

Fig. 4–4. Stop stitching about 2" from tip

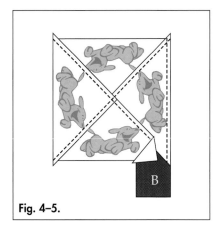

Fig. 4–5.

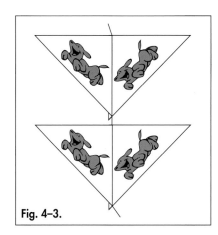

Fig. 4–6.

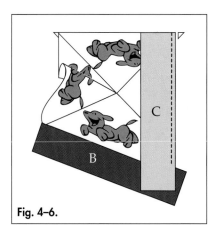

Fig. 4–7.

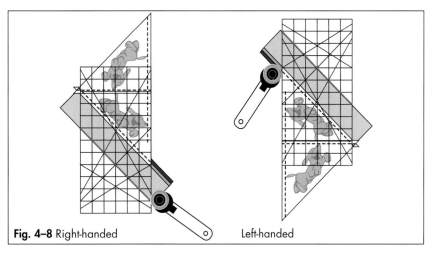

Fig. 4–8 Right-handed   Left-handed

Piecing the Novelty Windows Blocks (cont.)

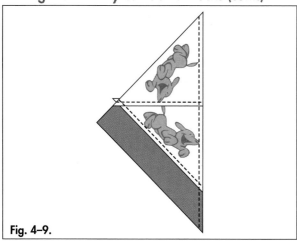

Fig. 4–9.

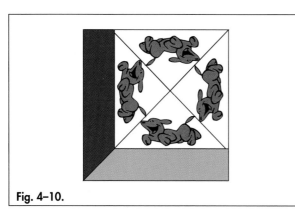

Fig. 4–10.

Assembling the Quilt

Sew a vertical sashing strip to the B rectangle on each block. Arrange the blocks in rows, following the quilt assembly diagram. Sew the vertical seams in each row, adding a vertical sashing strip to the right end of each row. Measure the width of the rows and cut the horizontal sashing strips to this measurement. Sew the rows together, adding the horizontal sashing strips between the rows and at the top and bottom of the quilt.

Adding the Borders

The borders have butted corners. From the accent border fabric, cut four 1" strips across the fabric width. Sew the strips together, end to end, before cutting the border lengths. Measure the quilt top down the center and cut 2 border strips this length. Sew the strips to the long sides. Measure across the width in the center of the quilt, including borders, and cut 2

border strips this length. Sew them to the top and bottom.

For the outer border, cut five 3½" strips across the width, or four 48" lengthwise strips. For borders cut across the width, piece the strips of each color together into one long strip. Measure, cut, and sew as for the first border.

Finishing the Quilt

Prepare the backing by piecing together two 1⅜-yard lengths of backing fabric. Layer the quilt top, batting, and backing. Quilt the layers and bind the raw edges.

Quilting Notes

The window frames, sashing, and borders are quilted in the seam lines. Two additional rows of straight quilting finish the outer border. In each window, free-motion quilting outlines the figures and fills the background.

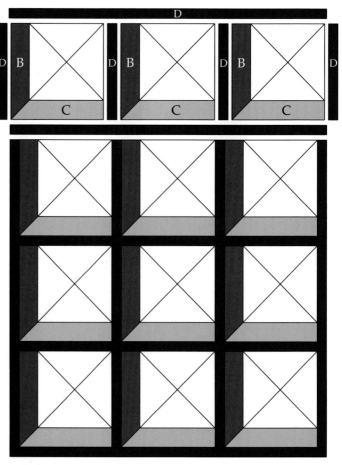

Quilt assembly.

ARGYLE DIAMONDS
29½" x 46", made by the author.

detail ARGYLE DIAMONDS

ARGYLE DIAMONDS

Finished Quilt Top: 29½" x 46"
Finished Block: 7½" x 13"

Intermediate

The main fabric triangles in this quilt are a good size for medium-scale novelty prints and scenic prints. For Accent Fabric B, look for a fabric that is close to the ground color of the main fabric. Optional cording enhances the diamond shapes.

Fabric Requirements					
Measurements in yards unless otherwise indicated.					
If the design repeat of **Main Fabric A** is	6"–10"	11"–14"	15"–20"	21"–27"	over 27"
You will need this many yards	2¼	2⅞	3¾	5	6 repeats

Additional Fabrics	
Accent B – diamond triangle tips	⅜
Accent C – lighter diamonds	½
Accent D – darker diamonds	⅝
Narrow Accent Border	¼
Outer Border*	½ – pieced or 1⅜ – seamless
Backing	1½
Binding – cut 2½" strips crosswise	⅜

*The Main Fabric A yardage includes a pieced outer border. If you would like to use a different border fabric, this is the extra yardage you will need, but don't reduce the Main Fabric yardage.

Cutting Main Fabric A

Review the directions for selective cutting on pages 72–73. Use template A1, on page 129, for this design.

Stack-n-Select Chart for Argyle Diamonds Quilt		
Cut layers 21" wide. Cut 6 identical layers for each stack. Use a different set of identical layers for each additional stack.		
If the lengthwise design repeat is:	Use this many design repeats for each layer:	Make this many stacks:
6"–14"	One repeat	1 or 2 as needed
Over 14"	One repeat	1
Selectively Whack...		
(9) 60° triangle block kits from one or two stacks using template H, centering a novelty print motif in each triangle		

See pages 112–114 for instructions on cutting 60° triangles, diamonds, and half-diamonds.

Cutting Fabrics B, C, and D		
Fabric and Position	**First Cut**	**Second Cut**
Diamond triangle tips B	(2) 4" strip across width	(18) 60° triangles
Accent C – lighter diamonds	(2) 3¾" strips across width	(12) 60° diamonds
Accent C – half-diamonds, sides	(2) 2⅜" strip across width	(12) 60° half-diamonds
Accent D – darker diamonds	(2) 3¾" strip across width	(12) 60° diamonds
Accent D – triangles, top and bottom	(2) 4" strip across width	(12) 60° triangles

Piecing the Argyle Diamond Blocks

Piece 9 Argyle Diamond blocks as follows:

Each stack of 6 identical triangles is a block kit. To keep from unintentionally turning a triangle, put a reference pin in each of the 6 triangles on the edge that you want to use for the outer edge of the hexagon. The opposite point will be at the center of the block (Fig. 4–11).

Fig. 4–11.

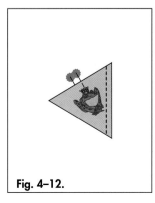

Fig. 4–12.

Pick up the first 2 triangles from a stack and sew them, right sides together, with the reference pins at the top left (Fig. 4–12, page 87).

Repeat with a second pair of triangles. Finger-press the seam allowances open (Fig. 4–13).

Sew one of the remaining triangles to each pair, matching the tips at the top and bottom. The reference pins should be on the same side.

Press the seam allowances open (Figs. 4–14 and 4–15).

You should have 2 identical halves. Remove the pins. Place the halves right sides together and sew across the center of the block, matching the seams at the center. Press these seam allowances open.

Add B triangles to 2 opposite sides of the

Piecing the Blocks

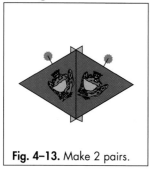
Fig. 4–13. Make 2 pairs.

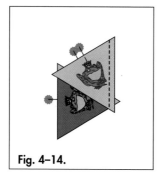
Fig. 4–14.

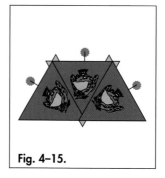
Fig. 4–15.

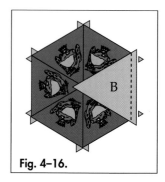
Fig. 4–16.

Fig. 4–17.

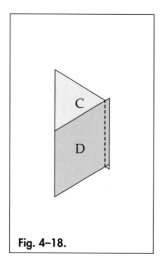
Fig. 4–18.

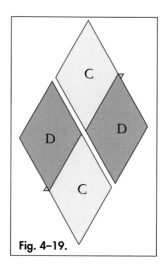
Fig. 4–19.

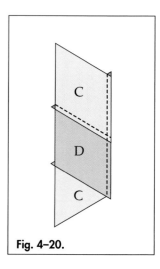
Fig. 4–20.

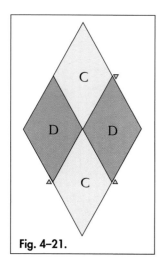
Fig. 4–21.

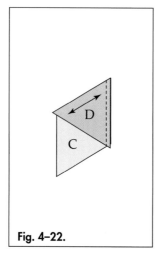
Fig. 4–22.

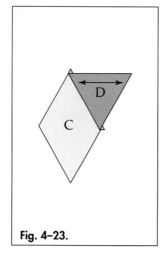
Fig. 4–23.

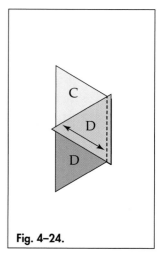
Fig. 4–24.

hexagon. Press the seam allowances toward the triangles (Figs. 4–16 and 4–17).

Piecing the Setting Blocks

Piece the setting blocks as follows:

For the diamond blocks, begin by making 8 pairs of C and D diamonds. Note that the triangle tips extend ¼" at each end of the seam line. Finger-press the seam allowances toward the D diamonds (Fig. 4–18).

Arrange two pairs with the C diamonds at the top and bottom (Fig. 4–19).

Flip the pair on the right over the left pair and sew, matching the seams at the center (Fig. 4–20).

Press the seam allowances to one side. Make 4 diamonds for the center of the quilt (Fig. 4–21).

For the 4 top and bottom setting triangles, use C diamonds and D triangles as follows:

Sew a Fabric D triangle to the top right edge of each diamond, placing the straight-grain edge of the triangle as shown by the arrow. The top corner of the triangle should line up with the tip of the diamond. The triangle will extend ¼" at the lower end. Finger-press the seam allowances toward the triangle (Figs. 4–22 and 4–23).

Turn the diamonds and add Fabric D triangles to the opposite sides, again aligning the tip of the triangle with the tip of the diamond. Carefully press the finished triangle units from the right side, pressing the seam allowances toward the triangles (Figs. 4–24 and 4–25).

For the 4 side setting triangles, use C half-diamonds and D diamonds:

Sew a diamond to a half-diamond as shown. The diamond tip extends ¼" past the half-diamond at the top. Finger-press the seam allowances toward the half-diamond (Fig. 4–26).

Sew a half-diamond to the adjacent side of the diamond. Press the seam allowances

Piecing the Blocks (cont.)

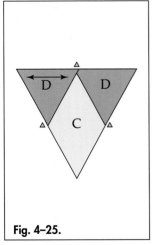

Fig. 4–25.

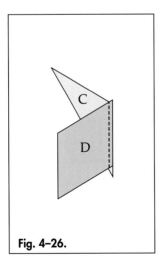

Fig. 4–26.

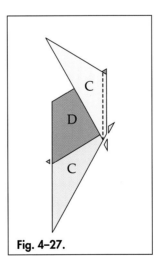

Fig. 4–27.

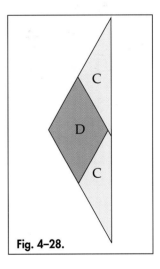

Fig. 4–28.

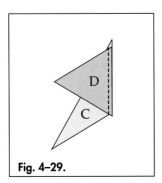

Fig. 4–29.

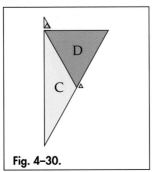

Fig. 4–30.

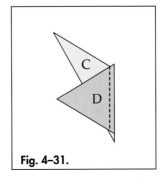

Fig. 4–31.

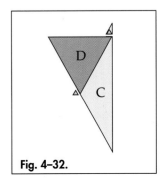

Fig. 4–32.

toward the half-diamond (Figs. 4–27 and 4–28, page 89).

Piece 4 corner setting triangles as follows:

Add D triangles to the top right edge of 2 C half-diamonds as shown. Press the seam allowances toward the triangles (Figs. 4–29 and 4–30, page 89).

Add D triangles to the lower right edge of 2 C half-diamonds. Press the seams toward the triangles (Figs. 4–31 and 4–32, page 89).

Assembling the Quilt

Arrange the blocks and the setting triangles according to the quilt assembly diagram. Piece the blocks together in diagonal rows, then sew the rows together.

If desired, add cording to the design. Lay the cording over the seam lines, outlining the Argyle Diamond blocks as shown in the quilt on page 85. Zigzag stitch over the cording. Use a tear-away stabilizer under the quilt top, if necessary, to prevent puckering. Extend the ends of the cording into the seam allowances at the edges of the quilt.

Adding the Borders

The borders have butted corners. From the accent border fabric, cut four 1" strips across width. Measure the quilt top down the center and cut 2 border strips this length. Sew the strips to the long sides. Measure across the width in the center of the quilt, including borders, and cut 2 border strips this length. Sew them to the top and bottom.

For the outer border, cut five 3½" strips across the width or four 3½" x 42" lengthwise strips. If you are using a directional print, such as a scenic print, you may want to have the design run in one direction. In that case, use lengthwise strips for the sides and cut the top and bottom borders across the width, piecing as necessary. For borders cut across the width, piece the strips of each color together into one

long strip. Measure, cut, and sew as for the first border.

Finishing the Quilt

Layer the quilt top, batting, and backing. Quilt the layers and bind the raw edges.

Quilting Notes

The borders and hexagonal block centers are quilted in the seam lines. Diagonal quilting lines form crosses in each of the setting blocks and follow alongside the cording.

Quilt assembly.

75" x 75", made by the author.

detail MEDALLION STAR

MEDALLION STAR

Finished Quilt Top: 75" x 75"
Finished Block: 20½"

Advanced Intermediate

Here is a classic design for you to try in a decorative stripe. The stripe does not need to be symmetrical, and floral striped designs are especially effective. Changing the values of the background and various accent fabrics can alter this block dramatically. After cutting the block kits, it's always a good idea to experiment with a few pieces on a design wall before cutting up all the other fabrics.

Fabric Requirements					
Measurements in yards unless otherwise indicated.					
If the design repeat of **Main Fabric A** is	6"–10"	11"–14"	15"–20"	21"–27"	over 27"
You will need this many yards	5	3½	5	6⅝	8 repeats

Additional Fabrics	
Background B – cream	2¼
Accent C – medium gold triangles	¾
Accent D – dark gold triangles	½
Accent E – yellow diamonds	½
Sashing and Border – red	2¼
Side Setting Triangles – navy	1½
Backing – pieced lengthwise	4¾
Binding – cut 2½" strips crosswise	⅝

Cutting Main Fabric A

Review the directions for selective cutting on pages 72–73. Use templates M1 and M2 (page 130) for this design.

Stack-n-Select Chart for Medallion Star Quilt		
Cut layers 21" wide. Cut 8 identical layers for each stack. Use a different set of identical layers for each additional stack.		
If the lengthwise design repeat is:	Use this many design repeats for each layer:	Make this many stacks:
6"–10"	Two repeats	2
11"–14"	One repeat	2
Over 14"	One repeat	1
Selectively Whack...		
(5) 45° triangle block kits using template M1		▲
(5) trapezoid block kits using template M2		▼

Cutting the Additional Block Fabrics

This block will be easier to piece and more likely to lie flat if you pay careful attention to the grain lines when cutting and piecing. Label the quarter-square and half-square triangles and keep them separate because they may be difficult to tell apart. The block piecing illustrations and block diagram show the positioning of the two types of triangles.

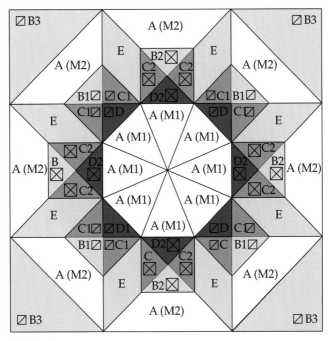

Fabric placement.

Cutting Additional Block Fabrics

Fabric	Position	First Cut	Second Cut	Third Cut
Background B	B1: Half-square Triangles	(1) 3⅜" strip across width	(10) 3⅜" squares	Cut each square once on the diagonal to make (20) half-square triangles
Background B	B2: Quarter-square Triangles	(1) 4¾" strip across width	(5) 4¾" squares	Cut each square twice on the diagonal to make (20) quarter-square triangles
Background B	B3: Large Half-square Triangles – corner	(2) 6⅞" strips across width	(10) 6⅞" squares	Cut each square once on the diagonal to make (20) half-square triangles
Accent C	C1: Half-square Triangles	(2) 3⅜" strips across width	(20) 3⅜" squares	Cut each square once on the diagonal to make (40) half-square triangles
Accent C	C2: Quarter-square Triangles	(2) 4¾" strips across width	(10) 4¾" squares	Cut each square twice on the diagonal to make (40) quarter-square triangles
Accent D	D1: Half-square Triangles	(1) 3⅜" strip across width	(10) 3⅜" squares	Cut each square once on the diagonal to make (20) half-square triangles
Accent D	D2: Quarter-square Triangles	(1) 4¾" x 24" strip	(5) 4¾" squares	Cut each square twice on the diagonal to make (20) quarter-square triangles
Accent E	E: Star Diamonds	(5) 3" strips across width	(40) 3" diamonds	

Piecing the Medallion Star Block

Use one M1 block kit and one M2 block kit for each block. Piece 5 Medallion Star blocks as follows:

Center Square

Place the M1 wedges together in pairs. To match any stripes in the pattern, "stick-pin" at a couple of points along the seam edge, or "peek and pinch" as you sew the seam. Finger-press the seam allowances open (Figs. 4–33, 4–34, and 4–35).

Use a ¼" seam allowance to sew 4 pairs into quarter-blocks. Finger-press the seam allowances open. Join the quarter-blocks to make half-blocks. Press the seam allowances

Piecing the Center Square

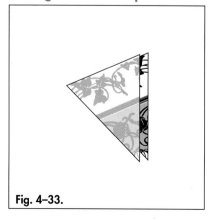

Fig. 4–33.

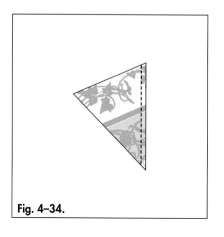

Fig. 4–34.

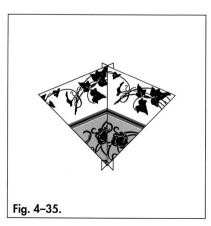

Fig. 4–35.

Cutting Setting Fabrics

Fabric	Position	First Cut	Second Cut	Third Cut
Background B	Sashing	(16) 1¾" strips across width	(32) 1¾" x 21" strips	
Accent C	Small cornerstones	(1) 1¾" strip across width	(20) 1¾" squares	
Accent C	Small half-cornerstones	(1) 2⅛" strip across width	(8) 2⅛" squares	Cut each square once on the diagonal to make (16) half-square triangles
Accent D	Large cornerstones	(1) 2½" x 20" strip	(8) 2½" squares	
Accent D	Large half-cornerstones strip	(1) 2⅞" x 12" strip	(4) 2⅞" squares	Cut each square once on the diagonal to make (8) half-square triangles
Sashing	Sashing and border	(4) 2½" x 72" lengthwise strips for border	(2) 23½" strips across remaining width	(16) 2½" x 23½" strips for sashing
Setting triangles	Side quarter-square triangles	(1) 30¼" strip across width	(1) 30¼" square	Cut the square twice on the diagonal to make (4) quarter-square triangles
Setting triangles	Corner half-square triangles	(1) 15⅜" strip across width	(2) 15⅜" squares	Cut each square once on the diagonal to make (4) half-square triangles

open. Sew the center seam. Press the seam allowances open and steam-press the finished octagon, blocking it a bit if necessary (Fig. 4–36).

Add D1 triangles to four sides to create a square. Press the seam allowances away from the center (Figs. 4–37 and 4–38).

Peek and Pinch

Use this method to align stripes without pinning. With the sewing machine needle in the down position, lift the top fabric and align the stripes immediately in front of the presser foot. Then hold the two layers in place with your fingers, a pin tip, or a stiletto as you sew.

Piecing the Center Square (cont.)

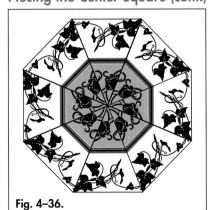

Fig. 4–36.

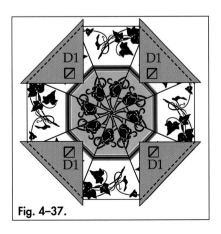

Fig. 4–37.

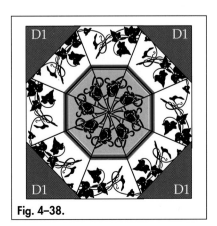

Fig. 4–38.

Star Point Units

The star points are made as left and right units. Note that the grain lines of the triangles are placed differently for the 2 units. Use half-square or quarter-square triangles as indicated by the symbols in the piecing and block assembly illustrations.

Left Units – Make 4 for each block.

With the right side of the diamond fabric facing up, sew a C2 triangle to the lower-right edge of 4 diamonds, matching the triangle tip with the tip of the diamond. Press the seam allowances toward the accent triangle (Figs. 4–39 and 4–40).

Turn the diamonds so that the triangle is at the top left. Sew a C1 triangle to the top-right edge, aligning the tips as before. Press the seam allowances toward the accent triangle (Figs. 4–41 and 4–42).

Turn the diamond so that the accent triangles are on the right. Sew a D2 triangle to the C2 triangle, aligning the upper and right edges. Press the seam allowances toward the D2 triangle and trim off the tips (Figs. 4–43 and 4–44).

Right Units – Make 4 for each block.

With the right side of the diamond fabric facing up, sew a C1 triangle to the lower-right edge of 4 diamonds, matching the triangle tip with the tip of the diamond. Press the seam allowances toward the accent triangle (Figs. 4–45 and 4–46).

Turn the diamonds so that the triangle is at the top left. Sew a C2 triangle to the top-right edge, aligning the tips. Press the seam allowances toward the accent triangle and trim off the tips (Figs. 4–47 and 4–48).

Piecing the Left Star Point Unit

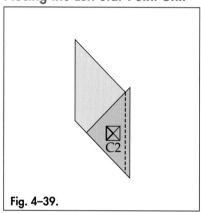

Fig. 4–39.

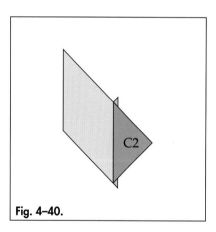

Fig. 4–40.

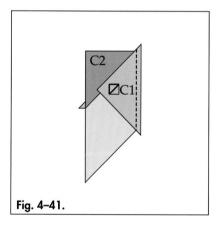

Fig. 4–41.

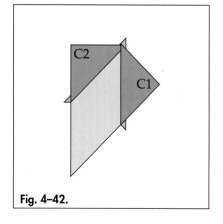

Fig. 4–42.

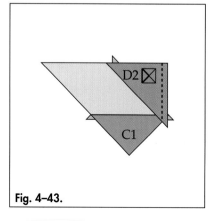

Fig. 4–43.

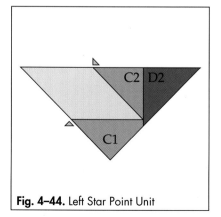

Fig. 4–44. Left Star Point Unit

M2/Background Quarter-Triangle Units

Sew a B2 triangle to the short straight edge of 4 of the M2 pieces. Press the seam allowances toward the M2 piece (Fig. 4–49).

Two-Point Units

Arrange the M2 triangle units and right star-point units as shown (Fig. 4–50).

Flip the star-point unit over onto a triangle unit and sew together. Press the seam allowances toward the star-point unit. Repeat with the other 3 units (Figs. 4–51 and 4–52).

Place this new unit with the left star-point unit as shown (Fig. 4–53).

Flip the right unit over onto the left unit, matching the seams. Sew together. Repeat with the other 3 units. Press the seam allowances toward the left units (Figs. 4–54 and 4–55).

Piecing the Right Star Point and Two-Point Unit

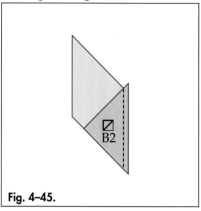

Fig. 4–45.

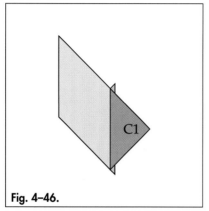

Fig. 4–46.

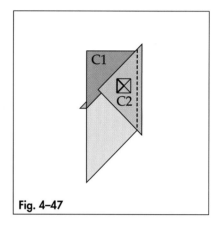

Fig. 4–47

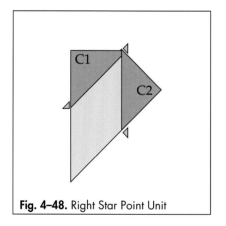

Fig. 4–48. Right Star Point Unit

Fig. 4–49.

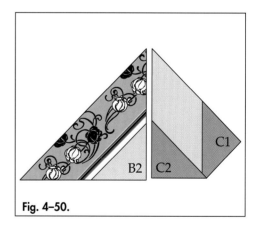

Fig. 4–50.

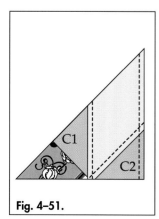

Fig. 4–51.

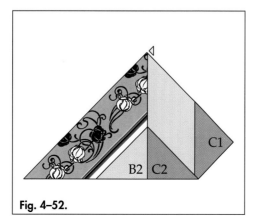

Fig. 4–52.

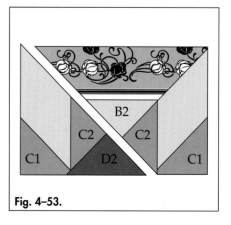

Fig. 4–53.

Corner Units

Sew a B1 triangle to the short straight edge of the remaining four M2 pieces. Sew a B3 triangle to the long side of the M2 pieces. Press the seam allowances toward the M2 piece (Fig. 4–56).

Assembling the Block

Arrange the center square, corner units, and two-point units as shown in the block assembly diagram.

Sew the corner triangles to the top and bottom two-point units, pressing the seam allowances toward the star points.

Sew the center block to the side two-point units, pressing the seam allowances toward the star points.

Sew the 3 rows together and press the seam allowances toward the star points. (Figs. 4–57)

Add the background sashing strips and small cornerstones to the blocks. Add sashing strips, small cornerstones, and small half-cornerstones to the side and corner setting triangles, as shown in the quilt assembly diagram.

Piecing the Blocks (cont.)

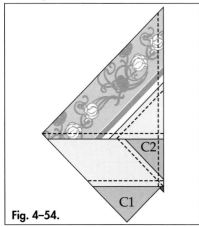

Fig. 4–54.

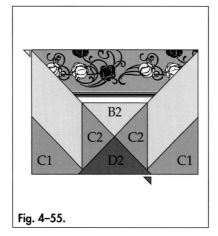

Fig. 4–55.

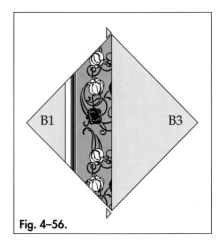

Fig. 4–56.

Fig. 4–57. Block assembly

Assembling the Quilt

Arrange the blocks, sashing, and setting pieces as shown in the quilt assembly diagram. Sew them together in diagonal rows, then sew the rows together.

Adding the Borders

The borders have butted corners. Measure the quilt top down the center and cut 2 border strips this length. Sew the strips to 2 opposite sides. Measure across the width in the center, including borders, and cut 2 border strips this length. Sew them to the remaining sides.

Finishing the Quilt

Prepare the backing by piecing together two 2½-yard lengths of backing fabric. Layer the quilt top, batting, and backing. Quilt the layers and bind the raw edges.

Quilting Notes

This quilt has a fleur-de-lis motif quilted in each block and in the borders. The pattern for the quilting is on page 131. Straight-line quilting anchors the sashing and borders, and free-motion stipple quilting fills the background areas around the blocks and quilted motifs.

Quilt assembly.

VENETIAN TILES
40" x 40", made by the author.

detail VENETIAN TILES

VENETIAN TILES

Finished Quilt Top: 40" x 40"
Finished Block: 10"

Advanced Intermediate

These elegant blocks with narrow strips of sashing recall leaded stained glass. For this wall quilt, the Stack-n-Select method was used to create maximum impact from a symmetrical print. For guidance in choosing a suitable main fabric, review pages 76–79.

Fabric Requirements
Measurements in yards unless otherwise indicated.

If the design repeat of **Main Fabric A** is	6"–10"	11"–14"	15"–20"	21"–27"	over 27"
You will need this many yards	5	6⅞	5	6⅝	8 repeats

Additional Fabrics	
Sashing B	1
Border C	1
Backing – pieced lengthwise	2⅝
Binding – cut 2½" strips crosswise	⅜

Cutting Main Fabric A

Review the directions for selective cutting on pages 72–79. Use templates V1 and V2 on page 128 for this design.

Stack-n-Select Chart for Venetian Tiles Quilt		
Cut layers 21" wide. Cut 8 identical layers for each stack. Use a different set of identical layers for each additional stack.		
If the lengthwise design repeat is:	Use this many design repeats for each layer:	Make this many stacks*:
6"–14"	Two repeats	2
Over 14"	One repeat	2
Selectively Whack...		
(9) 5½" 45° triangle block kits for octagonal tiles, placing the centerline of template V1 on an axis line. *Arrange as many wedges as possible on the first stack. If you are able to get all 9 from one stack, make the second stack for the corner triangles with just four layers. Otherwise, make the second stack with 8 layers to cut the necessary wedges, and then separate into four-layer stacks before cutting the triangles for the corner squares.		
(16) quarter-square triangle block kits for corner squares, placing the centerline of template V2 on an axis line		

Cutting Sashing Fabric B	
First Cut	**Second Cut**
(3) 5" strips across width	(112) 1" x 5" rectangles
(2) 5½" strips across width	(64) 1" x 5½" rectangles
(1) 6" strip across width	(16) 1" x 6" rectangles

Cutting Border Fabric C	
First Cut	**Second Cut**
(3) 5½" strips across width	(40) 5½" 45° triangle wedges – 14 per strip
(2) 6" strips across width	(16) 6" 45° triangle wedges – 12 per strip
See pages 110–111 for general instructions on cutting 45° wedges.	

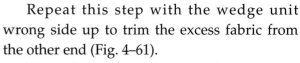

Piecing Venetian Tiles Blocks

Block Centers

Piece 9 Venetian Tiles block centers as follows: Work on one set of 8 identical wedges at a time.

Add a 1" x 5" rectangle to the short side of each wedge, centering the wedge on the rectangle. Finger-press the seam allowances toward the wedge (Figs. 4–58 and 4–59).

Place a ruler on the wedge with the 45-degree line on one long edge and the ruler edge on the other long edge. The ruler position may vary from the illustration, depending on the ruler design. Trim the excess fabric from the rectangle (Fig. 4–60).

Repeat this step with the wedge unit wrong side up to trim the excess fabric from the other end (Fig. 4–61).

Piece the wedge units together in pairs. Finger-press the seam allowances open (Figs. 4–62, 4–63, and 4–64).

Sew the pairs together into half-blocks. Finger-press the seam allowances open. Sew the halves together and press the seam allowances open (Fig. 4–65, page 104).

Piecing the Blocks

Fig. 4–58.

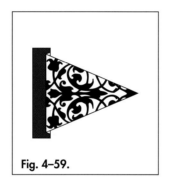

Fig. 4–59.

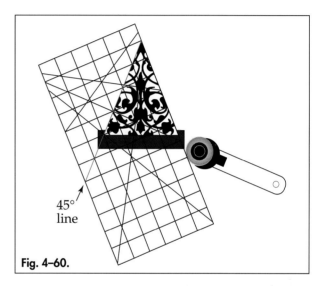

45° line

Fig. 4–60.

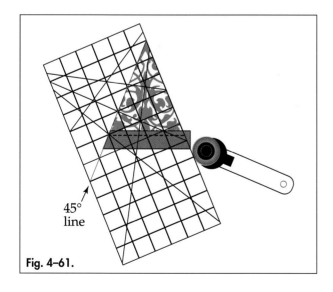

45° line

Fig. 4–61.

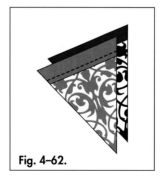

Fig. 4–62.

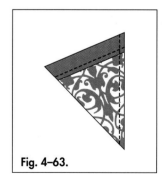

Fig. 4–63.

Fig. 4–64.

Block Corners

Piece 16 sets of block corners as follows: Work on one set of 4 identical triangles at a time (Fig. 4–66).

Add the 1" x 5½" rectangles to the long side of the corner triangles. Finger-press the seam allowances toward the triangle (Figs. 4–67 and 4–68).

Place a corner of a ruler (square or rectangular) on the tip of each triangle as shown and trim the excess fabric from one end (Fig. 4–69).

Repeat this step with each triangle unit turned wrong side up to trim the excess fabric from the other end (Fig. 4–70).

Do not sew these units to the block centers yet. Pin the sets of 4 together and set aside.

Border Block Units

Add the remaining 1" x 5½" rectangles to the 5½" border fabric wedges and trim as for the main-fabric wedge units (Fig. 4–71).

Add the 1" x 6" rectangles to the 6" border fabric wedges in the same manner. Cut the pieced wedges up the center as shown to make left and right half-wedges (Fig. 4–72).

Use these border units to piece 12 half-blocks for the side borders and 4 quarter-blocks for the corners (Figs. 4–73 and 4–74).

Piecing the Blocks (cont.)

Fig. 4–65.

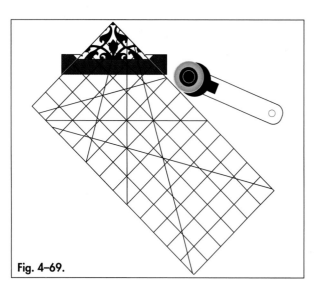

Fig. 4–69.

Piecing the Border Block Units

Fig. 4–66.

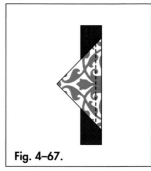

Fig. 4–67.

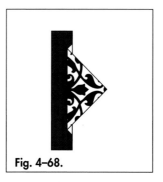

Fig. 4–68.

Fig. 4–70.

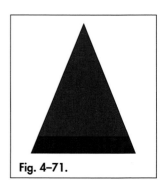

Fig. 4–71.

Assembling and Finishing the Quilt

Arrange the 9 block centers and the border blocks, following the quilt assembly diagram on page 106. Place sets of 4 corner triangles between the blocks.

Pin the corner triangles onto the adjacent centers. To keep the blocks in order and turned correctly, label each block as shown, using a piece of tape or an office label. The illustration shows the upper-left corner of the quilt (Fig. 4–75).

Add the corner triangles to each block to make them square. Press the seam allowances open or toward the corner triangle. Place each block back in position as you work.

In the same way, add the corner triangles to the border blocks.

Sew the vertical seams in each row, then sew the horizontal rows together.

Layer the quilt top, batting, and backing. Quilt the layers and bind the raw edges.

Piecing the Border Block Units

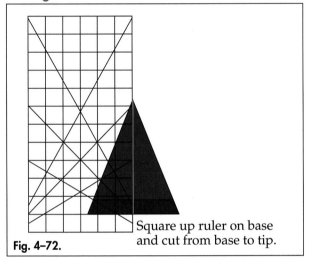

Square up ruler on base and cut from base to tip.

Fig. 4–72.

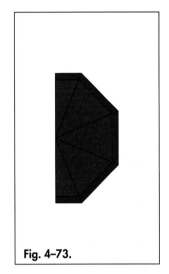

Fig. 4–73.

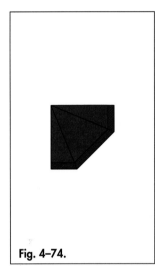

Fig. 4–74.

Fig. 4–75. Add the corner triangles to each block.

Finishing the Quilt

Prepare the backing by cutting the yardage in half and sewing the pieces together lengthwise. Layer the quilt top, batting, and backing. Quilt the layers and bind the raw edges.

Quilting Notes

Straight-line quilting in the accent fabric strips outlines the main fabric blocks. The octagonal block centers and square block corners are enhanced with free-motion quilting.

Quilt assembly.

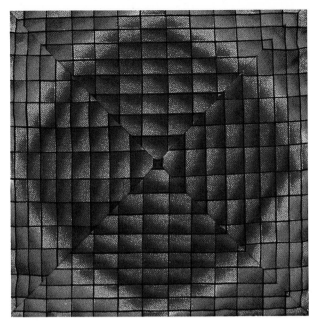

detail SECRET STAIRWAYS

PART FIVE:

General Instructions

The instructions in this section are written for right-handed sewers. The illustrations show both right-handed and left-handed positions.

Here are some guidelines for safe and accurate rotary cutting. If you are new to rotary cutting, practice on a few layers of scrap fabric until you are comfortable with the tools.

The cutter blade should be against the ruler and perpendicular to the mat, whether you cut right- or left-handed. Keep the cutter handle angled upward at about 45 degrees. If the angle is too low, the safety shield will interfere with cutting. If it is too high, it will be more difficult to control and potentially dangerous. If you have trouble keeping the ruler in place as you cut, try placing your pinkie off the far edge. You can also purchase small dots or squares of adhesive sandpaper to attach to your ruler.

For safety reasons, always cut away from your body. If the cutting angle is awkward, rearrange the fabric, turn the mat, or walk around the table so that you can cut safely. If you stand up and cut away from your body, your body weight will give you more leverage. Avoid sawing back and forth, which will result in jagged fabric edges. If you are not cutting through all the layers in one motion, try using more pressure. If the blade is skipping, leaving

a few threads uncut every few inches, it has a nick. Put in a new blade.

Close the safety shield every time you set the cutter down. In fact, it's best if you make a habit of closing the safety shield after every cut. This is a common-sense safety precaution, and it will also extend the life of your blades.

If you have trouble finding the ruler marks for a repetitive measurement, mark your ruler with tape or a removable marker. Wet-erase markers, available in office supply departments, are wonderful for marking rulers temporarily.

Most of the shapes used in these projects can be cut with any standard rotary-cutting ruler or a combination of a standard ruler and a temporary template. Some shapes are more easily cut with specialty rulers. See Sources on page 135 for more information on the specialty rulers shown in this section.

Cutting Strips
For Stack-n-Whack Block Kits

Cut and stack the repeats, following the instructions in Part One, beginning on page 7. The fabric should be unfolded and stacked with all layers right side up. To get a smooth edge, trim the right end of the fabric perpendicular to the fabric edge closest to you. Cut a strip across the width, using the strip-width

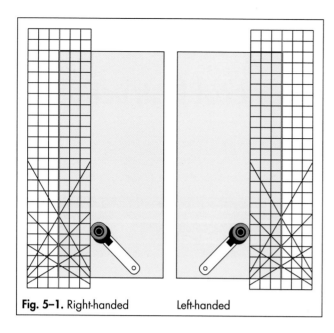

Fig. 5–1. Right-handed   Left-handed

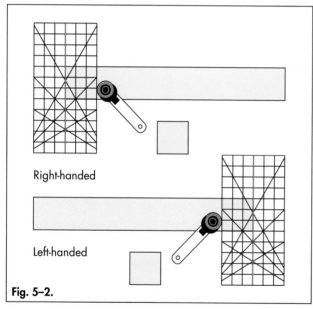

Right-handed

Left-handed

Fig. 5–2.

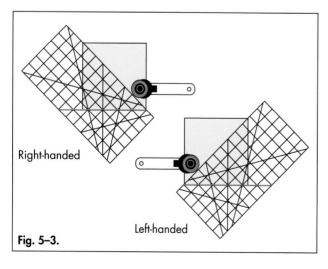

Right-handed

Left-handed

Fig. 5–3.

measurement in your project directions. Cut additional strips as needed, taking care that the cuts remain perpendicular to the fabric edge so the strips will be straight (Fig. 5–1).

For Background and Accent Fabrics

Unless otherwise directed in the instructions, begin with the fabric folded in half lengthwise, with selvages together. Trim the right end of the fabric to get a smooth edge, perpendicular to the fold. Use the strip-width measurement in your project directions to cut a strip across the width. Cut additional strips as needed, taking care that the cuts remain perpendicular to the fold.

Unfold the strips. You can stack several strips, if desired. If the fabric has a directional print, take care to maintain the print orientation when placing the strips together.

Cutting Squares

Trim the layers at one end of the strip set, cutting off any selvages. Carefully turn the strip set so the trimmed edge is to your left. Lay the ruler down and measure over from the left edge, using the same measurement you used for the strip width, and cut to make a square (Fig. 5–2).

Cutting Half-Square Triangles

Cut a square once on the diagonal, aligning the 45-degree line along one edge for greater accuracy. You will have two identical triangles with the straight of grain on the two short sides and a bias edge on the long side (Figs. 5–3 and 5–4).

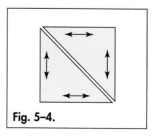

Fig. 5–4.

Cutting Quarter-Square Triangles

Cut a square twice on the diagonal, aligning the 45-degree line along one edge for greater accuracy. These cuts give you four identical triangles. Each triangle will have the straight of the grain on the long side and bias edges on the two short sides (Figs. 5–5 and 5–6).

Cutting 45-Degree Diamonds

On the right end of the strip set, lay the ruler down with the 45-degree line along one long edge. Because the placement of the 45-degree line varies on different brands of rulers, your ruler may be positioned differently from the one in the illustration. Place the edge of the ruler far enough in to avoid the selvages. Cut along the ruler's edge through all layers. Set aside this first cut, which is scrap fabric (Fig. 5–7).

Carefully turn the strip set around so the angled edge is to your left. Place the line used to measure the strip width (in this example, 3") on the angled edge, and the 45-degree line on one straight edge. Cut to make the diamond (Fig. 5–8).

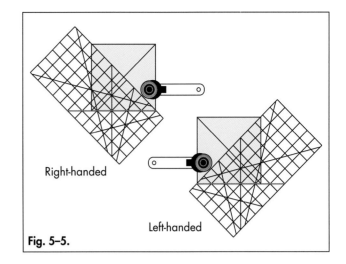

Right-handed

Left-handed

Fig. 5–5.

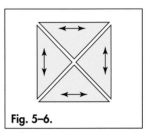

Fig. 5–6.

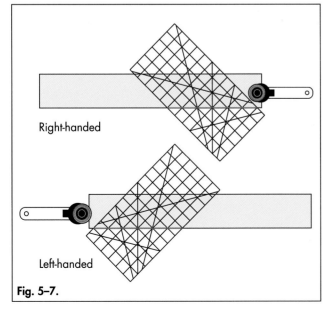

Right-handed

Left-handed

Fig. 5–7.

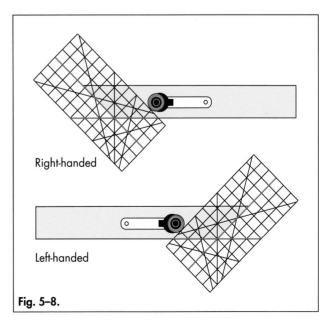

Right-handed

Left-handed

Fig. 5–8.

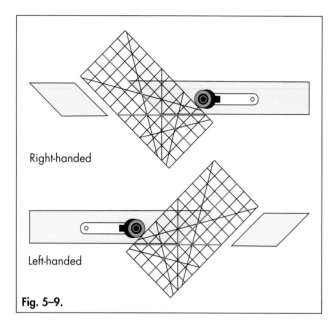

Right-handed

Left-handed

Fig. 5–9.

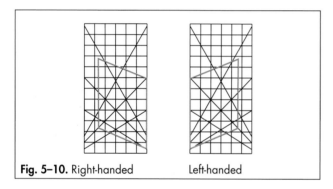

Fig. 5–10. Right-handed   Left-handed

To cut additional diamonds, do not turn the strip. Slide the ruler along the long edge and align the 45-degree line and the strip width measurement line for each cut (Fig. 5–9).

Cutting 45-Degree Triangle Wedges
Method One: Template

Prepare the template on page 123 for the block size you're using in one of the following ways:

Trace the guide as accurately as possible on clear template plastic. Cut out the plastic cutting guide. With clear tape, attach the cutting guide to the underside of your ruler, with the right edge of the guide aligned with the right edge of the ruler. Or, you can lay your ruler over the template with the right edge of the ruler on the right edge of the guide and mark the guidelines on the ruler with a marker or tape. Use a wet-erase marker so it doesn't rub off on your fabric (Fig. 5–10).

Lay the ruler with the cutting guide down on the strip set, with the top and bottom edges of the guide aligned with the edges of the strip. Place the edge of the ruler far enough in to avoid the selvages. Cut along the edge through all layers. Set aside this first cut, which is scrap fabric (Fig. 5–11).

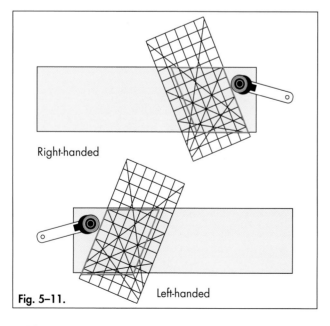

Right-handed

Left-handed

Fig. 5–11.

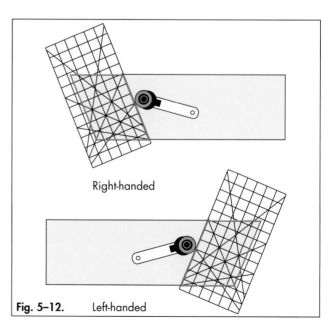

Right-handed

Fig. 5–12.   Left-handed

Carefully turn the strip set around so the angled edge is to your left. Lay the ruler down with the left edge of the cutting guide on the angled edge and cut. For additional wedges, slide the ruler and continue cutting double-triangles (Fig. 5–12).

Align the 45-degree line of your ruler with the cut edge of the piece and cut diagonally to make two 45-degree wedges (Figs. 5–13 and 5–14).

Method Two: Acrylic Tool

Place the tool on the strip set with the correct lines for the strip width aligned with the long edges. The illustrations show a 4" strip. Place the edge of the tool far enough in to remove the selvages and cut. The cut-off end of the strip is scrap fabric (Fig. 5–15). (See Sources, page 135, for the Stack-n-Whack 45-Degree Triangle Tool.)

Slide the tool over. Align the long edges of the strip with the width lines on the tool and place the angled edge on the corresponding angled line. Cut to make double-triangles (Fig. 5–16).

To cut the double-triangles into pairs of 45-degree triangle wedges, align the dotted placement line with the edge of the strip as shown and cut from corner to corner (Figs. 5–17 and 5–18).

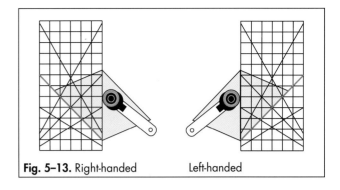

Fig. 5–13. Right-handed   Left-handed

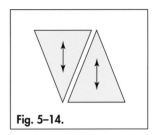

Fig. 5–14.

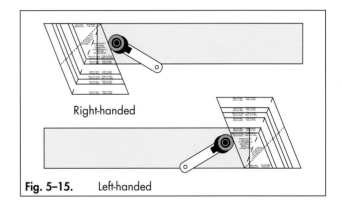

Right-handed

Fig. 5–15.   Left-handed

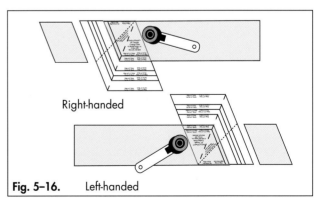

Right-handed

Fig. 5–16.   Left-handed

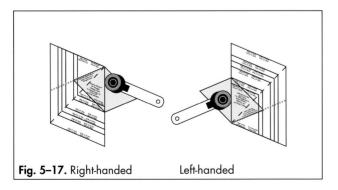

Fig. 5–17. Right-handed   Left-handed

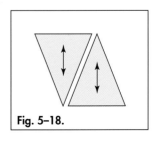

Fig. 5–18.

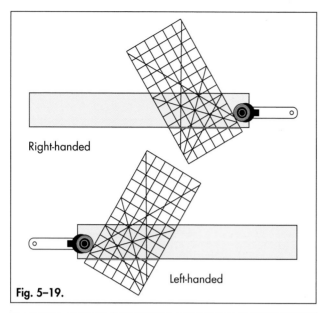

Fig. 5–19.

Right-handed

Left-handed

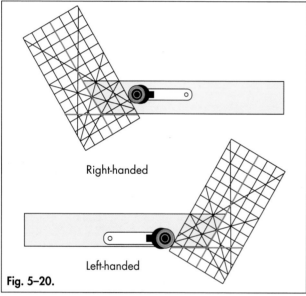

Right-handed

Left-handed

Fig. 5–20.

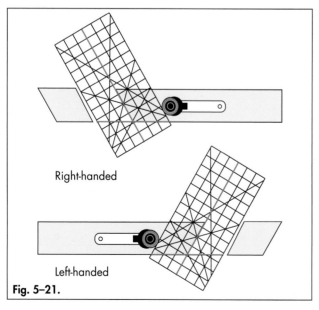

Right-handed

Left-handed

Fig. 5–21.

Cutting 60-degree Diamonds

On the right end of the strip set, lay the ruler down with the 60-degree line along one long edge. Because the placement of the 60-degree line varies on different brands of rulers, your ruler may be positioned differently from the one in the illustration. Place the edge of the ruler far enough in to avoid the selvages. Cut along the edge through all layers. Set aside this first cut, which is scrap fabric (Fig. 5–19).

Carefully turn the strip set around so the angled edge is to your left. Place the line used to measure the strip width (in this example, 3") on the angled edge, and the 60-degree line on one straight edge. Cut to make the diamond (Fig. 5–20).

To cut additional diamonds, do not turn the strip. Slide the ruler along the long edge and align the 60-degree line and the strip-width measurement line for each cut (Fig. 5–21).

Cutting 60-degree Triangles
Method One:
Rectangular Ruler with 60-Degree Line

Follow the directions for cutting 60-degree diamonds. For Stack-n-Whack block kits, place a reference pin in both straight-grain edges of each diamond. Cut the diamond in half, using the 60-degree line along one edge for greater accuracy (Figs. 5–22, 5–23, and 5–24).

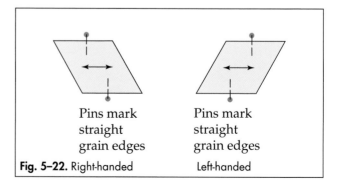

Pins mark straight grain edges

Pins mark straight grain edges

Fig. 5–22. Right-handed   Left-handed

Method Two:
Super 60™ or 60-Degree Triangle Ruler

Position the narrow end of the ruler at one edge of the strip and align the correct line for the strip width along the other edge. Cut along both sides of the triangle. For additional triangles, move the tool along the same edge, aligning the ruler with the last cut at the lower-right edge. For Stack-n-Whack block kits, place a reference pin in the straight-grain edges of each triangle set (Fig. 5–25). See Sources, page 135, for information on the Super 60 ruler.

Cutting 60-Degree Half-Diamonds
Method One: Template

Prepare a template using pattern A2 on page 129. Place the half-diamond template with the long side along one edge of the strip. Carefully cut along both sides of the template, using a ruler as a straight edge to protect the template. For additional half-diamonds, move the template along the same edge, aligning the right corner with the previous cut at the lower-right edge (Fig. 5–26).

Method Two: Super 60™ Ruler

Use the wide end of the Super 60 ruler (Sources page 135). Place the line for the strip width on one edge. Cut along both sides (Fig. 5–27).

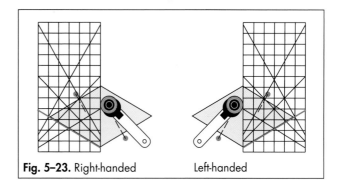

Fig. 5–23. Right-handed   Left-handed

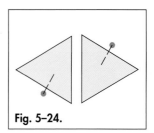

Fig. 5–24.

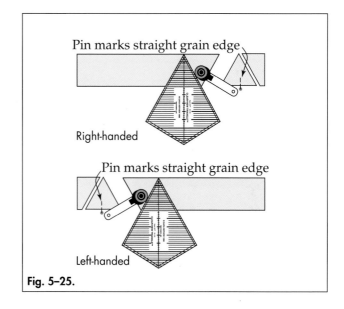

Pin marks straight grain edge

Right-handed

Pin marks straight grain edge

Left-handed

Fig. 5–25.

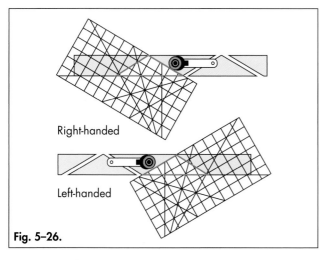

Right-handed

Left-handed

Fig. 5–26.

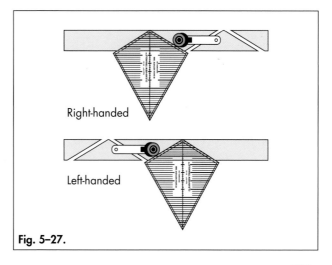

Right-handed

Left-handed

Fig. 5–27.

Method Three: 60-Degree Triangle Ruler

Align the center line of the ruler with the edge of the strip set to cut the first side. Turn the ruler and align the center line on the strip edge again to cut the second side (Fig. 5–28 and 5–29).

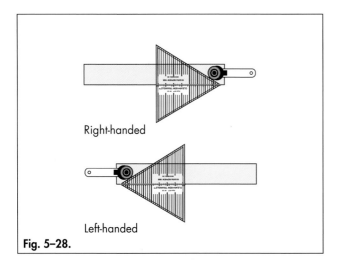

Right-handed

Left-handed

Fig. 5–28.

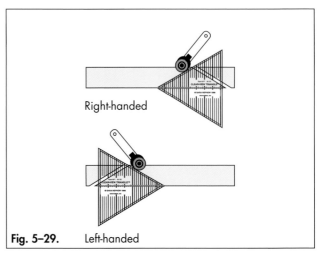

Right-handed

Fig. 5–29. Left-handed

Machine Piecing and Pressing

For quilters who have had limited experience with machine piecing, here are some basic tips.

A ¼" seam allowance should be used for all the piecing in the projects. There are a number of ways to increase the accuracy of your seam allowance width. Quarter-inch presser feet are available for almost all sewing machines, and they are a good investment. Many sewing machines also have an adjustable needle position, and you may be able to use this feature to obtain a ¼" seam allowance with your favorite presser foot. To check the accuracy of your seam allowance, cut four 2" x 4" strips of fabric and sew them together, side by side. Press the seam allowances and measure the total width of the set. It should be 6½". If it isn't, try again with another set of four strips, adjusting the width of your seam allowance until you get a 6½" set. Then make note of the needle position or mark the ¼" position on your sewing machine plate with a permanent marker, a piece of masking tape, or adhesive moleskin to serve as a guide. If you prefer, you can purchase one of the metal seam guides, available at fabric and quilt shops.

ONE CAVEAT: The finished measurement of a pieced unit can vary depending on how you press the seams. You may need to adjust your seam allowance accordingly, taking an exact or generous ¼" for seam allowances that will be pressed open and a scant ¼" for seam allowances that will be pressed to one side, because the folded edge or "turn of the cloth" tends to reduce the finished width a little bit. The variance may be only a needle's width, but it can make a difference on more complex blocks.

As you piece, be careful to keep a consistent seam allowance. Avoid veering off at the end of the seam.

Match pieces at the beginning and end of the seam. If you find that one piece ends up longer than the other, pin or hold the bottom edges together securely and ease the seam as you sew.

When you are joining two pieced units, try using the "dog ears" (the triangle tips that stick out past the seam allowance) to help match the seams. After sewing the seam, trim the tips with scissors or a rotary cutter before pressing. In the piecing illustrations, clipped tips are shown as small triangles set off a little from the pieced unit (Fig. 5–30).

However, if you are using a seam guide accessory or a ¼" foot that has a guide blade, you may find it necessary to trim the tips before sewing the seams.

To match seams that cross, try using a positioning pin. Push the pin through one block unit from the wrong side, exactly where the seam allowances cross from the previous sewing step. Push the pin through the matching point on the other block unit and bring the two units together. Hold the pin perpendicular to the fabric; do not bring it back up through the fabric. Place another pin about ¼" away from the positioning pin. Pin this one flat against the fabric as you normally would. Repeat with a third pin on the other side of the matching point. Remove the positioning pin and sew the seam. Remove the pins just before the presser foot reaches them or "walk" your machine over them one stitch at a time (Figs. 5–31 and 5–32).

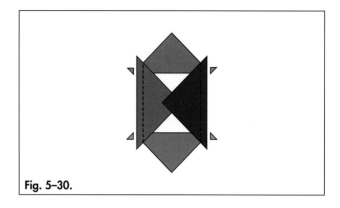

Fig. 5–30.

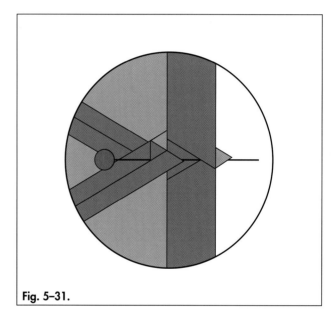

Fig. 5–31.

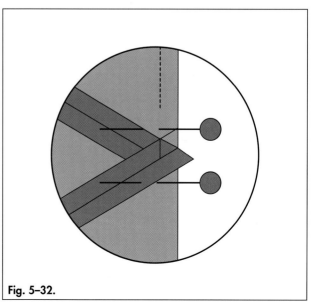

Fig. 5–32.

Pressing Covers a Multitude of Sins

This was my mother's dressmaking axiom, but I came to appreciate its wisdom when I learned to quilt. While careful pressing can improve almost any quilt, the reverse is unfortunately also true. Sloppy or over-zealous ironing can distort fabric, creating a multitude of piecing problems. If you missed out on "Pressing 101" in your formative years, seek out a quilting friend whose blocks always look neat and ask for a lesson. In the meantime, here are some suggestions that I have found helpful.

Before cutting your pieces, spray the fabric with sizing or spray starch and press until dry. This step accomplishes several things. By getting the fabric as smooth as possible, you will be able to cut the quilt pieces more accurately. A crisp, sized finish will make finger pressing easier, and the sized fabric will be less likely to stretch or distort during piecing.

During block construction, finger press whenever possible to reduce the chance of distortion. Place the fabric on a firm surface and use a fingernail or a small "wooden iron" to crease the seam. If pressing is necessary, use a dry iron. Steam and bias edges are incompatible. It is safer to save the steam until all the bias edges in a pieced unit have been stabilized in a seam line. To give a finished block a smooth, crisp appearance, use a little steam and spray sizing, and press from the right side on a terry towel.

Machine Appliqué

Preparing Appliqué Pieces

Two methods of preparing and positioning the pieces for machine appliqué are presented. You may use another favorite method if you like. If you prefer to appliqué by hand, remember to add a turn-under allowance to each piece as you cut it.

Paper-Backed Fusing Web Method: For best results with fusible web, prewash and press all background and appliqué fabrics.

This method is quick and simple. It stabilizes the fabrics for machine appliqué and helps to keep the raw fabric edges secure. You can use any brand of paper-backed fusing web.

Trace the appliqué shapes onto the paper side of the fusing web. The designs in this book are symmetrical, so you will not need to reverse them. If you are using this method with asymmetrical shapes, keep in mind that the finished shape will be a mirror image of the traced shape. Cut the tracings apart, leaving a margin of paper around each shape. Do not cut on the lines yet.

Fuse the paper-backed web to the wrong side of the appliqué fabric. Follow the manufacturer's instructions carefully because brands vary greatly in application requirements. Cut the appliqué pieces on the traced lines.

For strips, such as the stems for the MEADOW FLOWERS quilt, save time by fusing a rectangle of web to the wrong side of the appliqué fabric. Peel off the paper backing and cut the strips with a rotary cutter and ruler.

Freezer-Paper Method: Because the raw edges are not permanently fused in place, this method is not as durable as the previous one. However, it eliminates the need for fusing web and produces appliqué that is soft and flexible, like hand appliqué.

You will need plastic-coated freezer paper for this technique. The plastic coating softens when the paper is ironed at a low setting, allowing the paper to adhere temporarily to fabric. You should be able to peel the paper off the fabric easily. Before beginning your project, test the freezer paper on a scrap of fabric to determine the correct temperature and length of time needed to achieve a temporary bond.

Trace the appliqué shapes on the dull, uncoated side of the freezer paper. Cut the tracings apart, leaving a margin of paper around each shape. Do not cut on the lines yet.

Place the freezer paper with the shiny side against the right side of the appliqué fabric. Press on the paper side with a dry iron at a low setting. The paper should adhere to the fabric. If it does not, set the temperature slightly higher and check again.

Cut out the appliqué pieces on the traced lines. If you leave the freezer paper on the appliqué pieces until they are in place on the block, they will be easier to handle.

Positioning the Appliqué

If you are using a light background fabric, you may be able to position the appliqué pieces by laying a tracing of the appliqué design underneath the background fabric square. If you cannot see through the background fabric, you can use a light box, or try the following method:

Trace the block design on a lightweight nonwoven material, such as non-fusible interfacing or a tear-away sewing stabilizer. The material should be thin enough to see the appliqué fabrics when they are placed under-

neath and should be able to withstand medium heat. Mark the center and placement lines and embroidery lines on the tracing.

Place the tracing over the background fabric block, centering the design. Pin at two adjacent corners. Lift the tracing and slide the appliqué pieces underneath. Adjust them until they are in position.

Fusing Web Method: Peel off the paper backing before positioning the pieces. Press lightly at a low setting to tack the pieces in place. Remove the tracing and press securely, following the fusing-web manufacturer's directions.

Freezer-Paper Method: Spray the back of each appliqué piece with fabric basting spray (see Sources, page 135) or use a small amount of glue stick on the back of each piece before positioning it. Finger press the pieces in place. Remove the tracing and carefully peel off the freezer paper from each piece. If any pieces move during this step, lay the tracing down again and adjust as necessary. Use a pressing cloth to smooth the pieces without disturbing the placement.

Stitching the Appliqué

Machine appliqué the blocks with a zigzag, satin stitch, blind hem, or blanket stitch. Use matching or invisible thread for a hand-appliquéd effect or use a decorative thread, if you prefer. If you aren't familiar with the appliqué settings for your sewing machine, check the owner's manual or consult your machine dealer for recommended stitches and setup. Do a test on scraps to find the settings you like best for stitch width, stitch length, and tension. Appliqué a sample shape or two to check your thread choices and stitch settings. If the stitching puckers, try using a tear-away stabilizer under the block.

Machine Embroidered Details

The antennae on the Butterflies quilt and on the appliqued butterflies on the MEADOW FLOWERS quilt are machine embroidered. A simple zigzag stitch, tapering in width, can be used for these. If you have decorative stitches on your machine, experiment with different ones and adjust the width and length to suit. Mark the antennae on the fabric with a removable marker. Experiment with thread and stitch choices on scrap fabric, and then embroider.

Quilting Suggestions

A thoughtfully chosen quilting design can transform a good quilt top into an outstanding quilt. Quilting creates dimension and texture through the play of light and shadow on the surface. Ideally, quilting design should not be an afterthought. You can begin thinking about your quilting plan while you are piecing the top. If you have not made any decisions by the time you are through with the piecing, try hanging the quilt top where you can study it for a while before you begin quilting.

Your choice of quilting design will depend on many factors, including the unique patterns of your blocks, the time you have available, and the tools, threads, and accessories at your disposal. You can choose to do hand quilting, machine-guided quilting, free-motion quilting, or some combination. You can use the quilting notes included with each project as a guide or use your own creative vision.

Blocks made with Stack-n-Whack techniques are inherently strong focal points. Because they usually contain both curved and straight-edged elements, the blocks have a natural balance. Against this competition, an elaborate, fussy quilting design may be a wasted effort, or it may even be distracting. Structural quilting in or alongside the seam lines may be all that is necessary for some projects. It is a good first step for most quilts.

To bring out the distinctive patterns in each block, you can quilt around the same part of the print in each segment of the block. SARA'S ROSES (detail, page 36) is quilted this way. Study each block before you quilt it to see what shapes you want to emphasize.

For an easy but effective approach, you can choose a basic symmetrical pattern and repeat it in each block. An example of this is found in ROUNDABOUT STARS (detail, page 60), which has concentric circles in each block.

If your quilt has large areas of background, such as seen in MEDALLION STAR (page 91), you may want to use a simple quilting motif in these areas. In other cases, all-over quilting will serve to compress the background areas so that the kaleidoscope blocks can assume the starring role they deserve.

Remember to include the borders in your quilting plan. A quilt that is heavily quilted in the center and sparingly quilted in the borders will not hang or drape properly. To prevent distortion, keep the quilting evenly distributed.

If you are quilting by machine, consider experimenting with some of the gorgeous decorative threads now available. These threads can help you get extra design mileage from work as well as the less-expensive all-over quilting, but the customer must specify this and pay accordingly. Discuss design ideas and ask for an estimate. A good quilting service can transform your unfinished Stack-n-Whackier quilt tops into beautiful quilts, so you can get them out of the closet and onto beds or walls where they can be fully appreciated.

Fig. 5–33.

Bindings, Sleeves, and Labels

Bindings

Bindings add strength to the edges of your quilt. A bias-cut binding is essential for quilts with curved edges. For quilts with straight edges, however, a straight-grain binding can be used, and this type is easier to handle than bias binding. You can use the same fabric as your outer border, or provide a little accent with a contrasting binding.

Cut your straight-grain binding strips on the lengthwise or crosswise grain of the fabric. For a ⅜" finished binding, cut 2½" strips. Piece together enough strips to make a continuous binding strip long enough to go around the perimeter of the quilt, including about 12" for

turning corners and finishing the ends.

Piecing the strips on the diagonal will stagger the seam allowances for a smoother binding. Trim the excess fabric, leaving ¼" seam allowances. Press the seam allowances open (Fig.5–34).

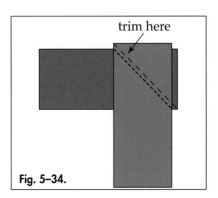

trim here

Fig. 5–34.

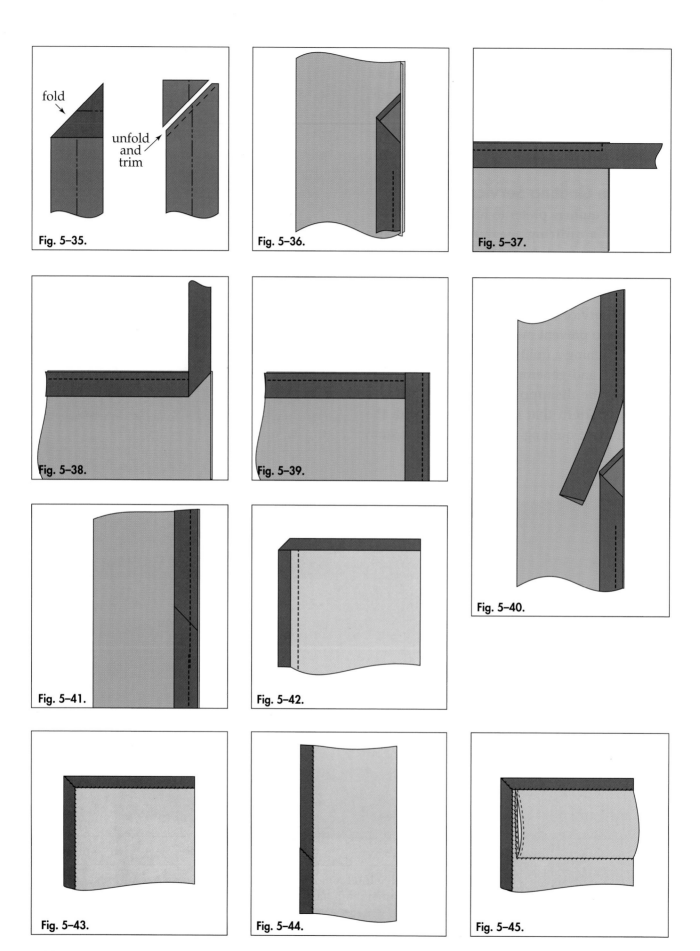

Fig. 5–35.

Fig. 5–36.

Fig. 5–37.

Fig. 5–38.

Fig. 5–39.

Fig. 5–40.

Fig. 5–41.

Fig. 5–42.

Fig. 5–43.

Fig. 5–44.

Fig. 5–45.

Press the long pieced binding strip in half lengthwise, wrong sides together. Press one end at a right angle and trim the extra fabric to ¼" from the fold line (Fig. 5–35).

If you want to add a sleeve for hanging your quilt, read the section about sleeves before attaching the binding.

To sew the binding, beginning part way down one side of your quilt, place the folded binding strip on the quilt top, right sides together and raw edges aligned. Leave about 3" unsewn at the beginning of the binding to allow for finishing. Sew the binding in place with a ⅜" seam allowance (on most machines, the width of the all-purpose presser foot will be about right) (Fig. 5–36).

As you approach each corner, stop stitching ⅜" from the raw edge of the quilt top at the corner. With the needle down, turn the quilt a quarter-turn. Backstitch straight back to the raw edge of the quilt and raise the needle and the presser foot (Fig. 5–37).

Fold the binding up at a 45-degree angle and then down, matching the second fold to the raw edge of the quilt. Begin stitching at the folded edge of the binding and continue to the next corner (Figs. 5–38 and 5–39).

When you come around to the first side again, stop stitching 3" or 4" from the beginning end. Lay the tail end along the raw edge, overlapping the beginning angled end and smooth the ends in place. Cut the tail end so that it overlaps the beginning end by ¼" to ½".

Tuck the tail end into the beginning end. Finish stitching the binding in place (Figs. 5–40 and 5–41).

Bring the folded edge of the binding around to the back and blindstitch it in place, tucking in the corners to form neat miters. Blindstitch the angled edge where the ends meet (Figs. 5–42, 5–43, and 5–44).

Sleeves

If you plan to hang your quilt or enter it in a show, consider adding a hanging sleeve as you sew the binding. This method saves time and results in a sleeve that will evenly distribute the weight of the quilt.

Prepare the sleeve by cutting a rectangle of fabric that is about 2" shorter than the width of the quilt. The rectangle width should be about 12" for bed quilts. For small wall quilts, 8" will suffice. Hem the short ends of the sleeve and press it in half lengthwise, wrong sides together.

Attach the binding to the front of the quilt, but don't bring the folded edge around to the back yet. On the back of the quilt, center the sleeve along the top edge and pin it in place. Stitch it to the quilt with a scant ⅜" seam allowance, just inside the seam line for the binding. Bring the binding around to the back and finish as directed previously, catching in the sleeve and the quilt back as you finish the top edge.

Blindstitch the lower layer of the sleeve ends and the folded edge of the sleeve to the quilt back (Figs. 5–45).

Labels

Label your quilt with your name, the date, and any other information you feel is important. If the quilt is to be a gift, you may want to add information about caring for the quilt. If the quilt will be exhibited, as a security measure, consider labeling the quilt in permanent ink underneath a sewn fabric label. Labels can be as simple or elaborate as you like. Your descendants and future quilters will be grateful that you provided this information.

GUIDES and PATTERNS

detail SECRET STAIRWAYS

Butterflies

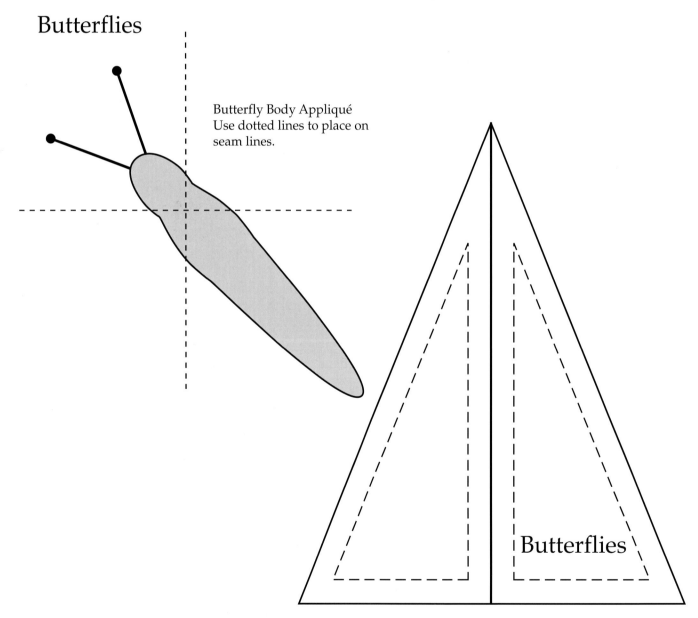

Butterfly Body Appliqué
Use dotted lines to place on
seam lines.

Butterflies

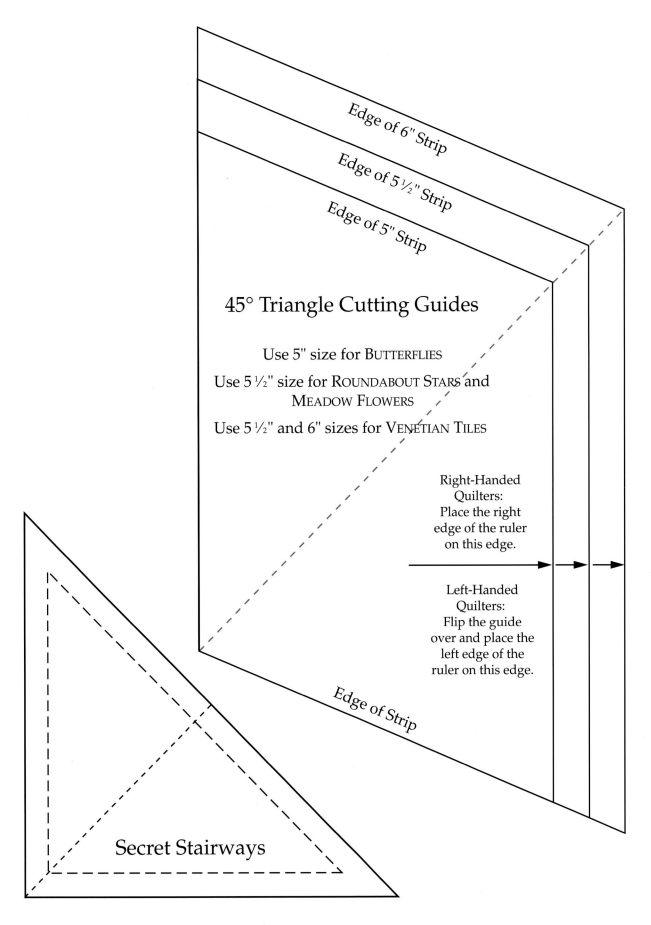

Edge of 6" Strip

Edge of 5 ½" Strip

Edge of 5" Strip

45° Triangle Cutting Guides

Use 5" size for BUTTERFLIES

Use 5 ½" size for ROUNDABOUT STARS and
MEADOW FLOWERS

Use 5 ½" and 6" sizes for VENETIAN TILES

Right-Handed
Quilters:
Place the right
edge of the ruler
on this edge.

Left-Handed
Quilters:
Flip the guide
over and place the
left edge of the
ruler on this edge.

Edge of Strip

Secret Stairways

Meadow Flowers
Six-Leaf Block
Placement Guide

Seam line

Place leaves first, then stem.
Add calyx last, overlapping
the seam line.

Center line of block

Calyx
Cut 18

Extend stem to lower edge of
10½" x 9½" rectangle

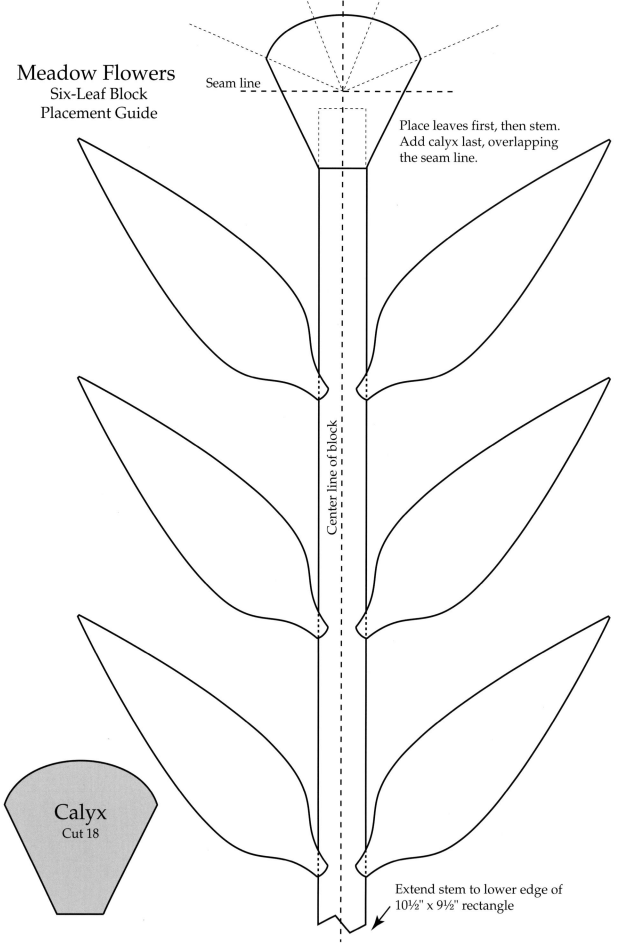

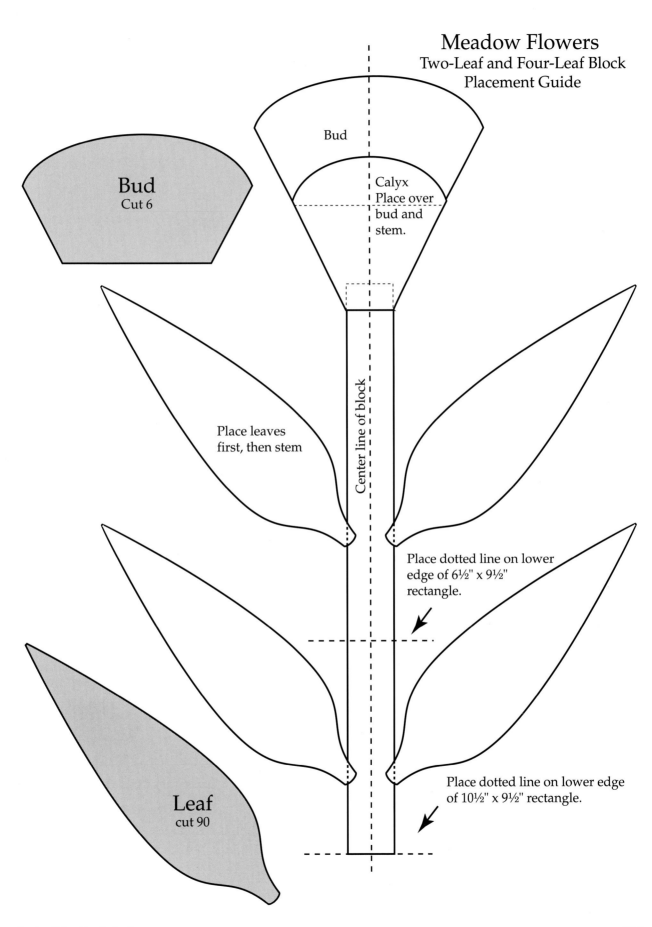

Meadow Flowers
Two-Leaf and Four-Leaf Block
Placement Guide

Bud

Calyx
Place over
bud and
stem.

Bud
Cut 6

Center line of block

Place leaves
first, then stem

Place dotted line on lower
edge of 6½" x 9½"
rectangle.

Place dotted line on lower edge
of 10½" x 9½" rectangle.

Leaf
cut 90

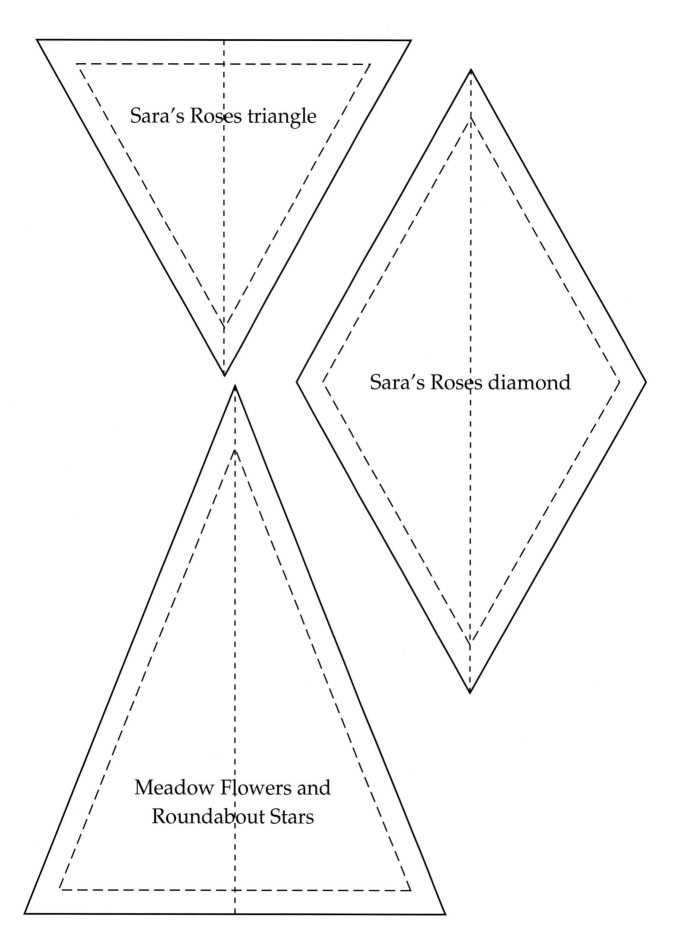

Sara's Roses triangle

Sara's Roses diamond

Meadow Flowers and
Roundabout Stars

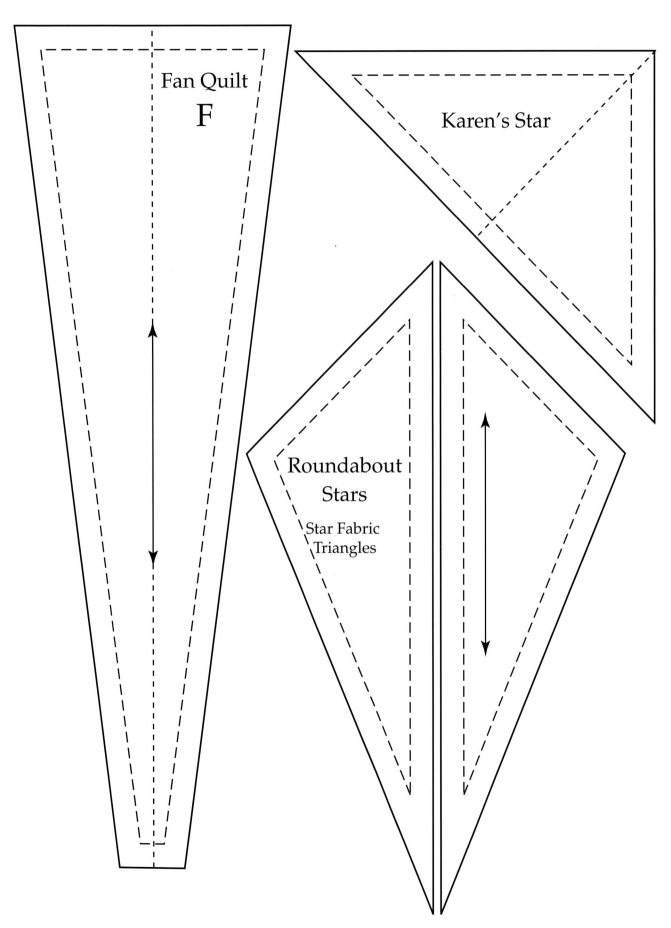

Fan Quilt
F

Karen's Star

Roundabout
Stars

Star Fabric
Triangles

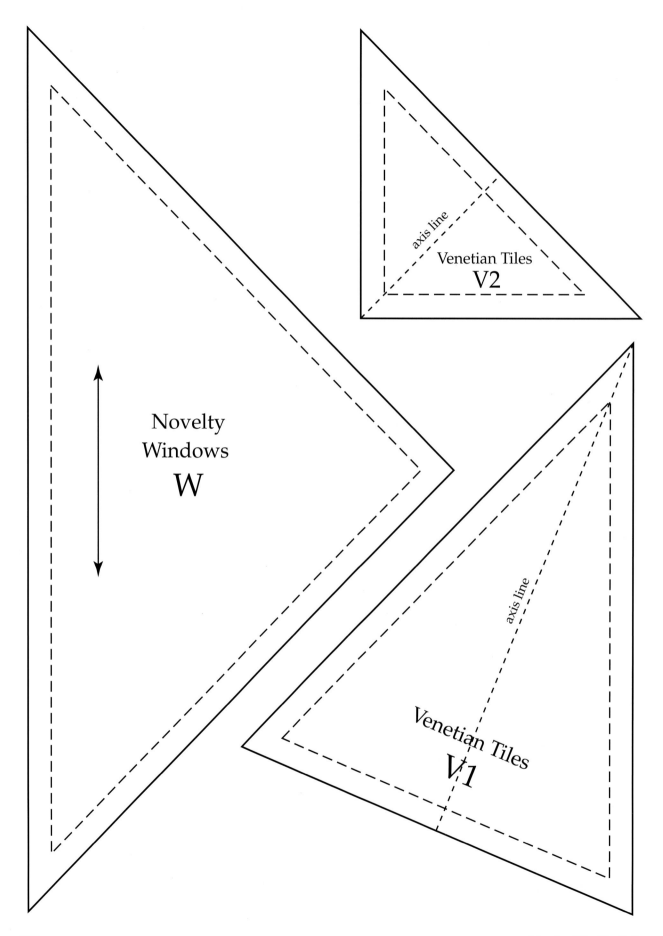

Novelty
Windows
W

Venetian Tiles
V2

axis line

Venetian Tiles
V1

axis line

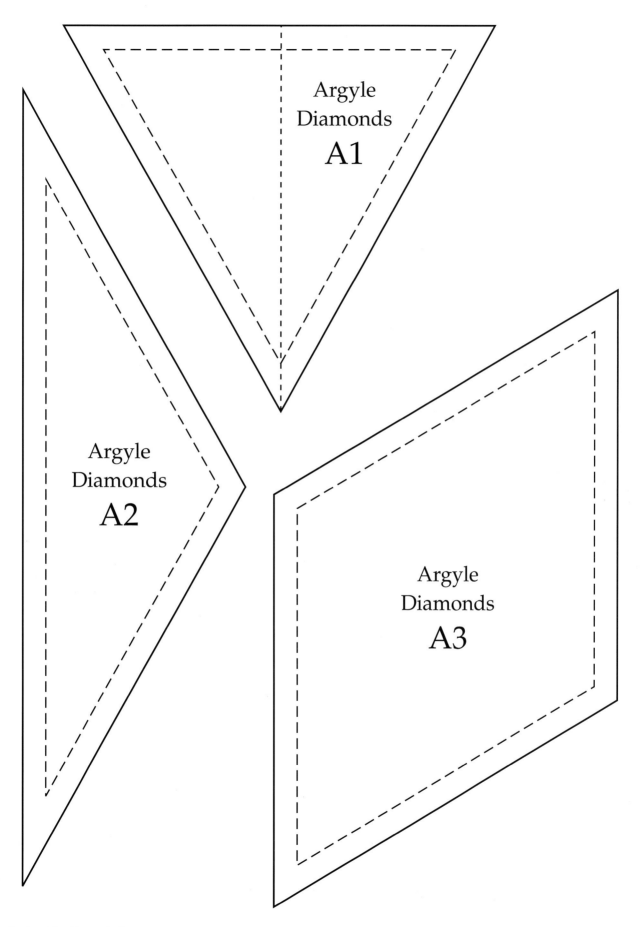

Argyle
Diamonds
A1

Argyle
Diamonds
A2

Argyle
Diamonds
A3

Medallion Star
M1

Run stripes in this direction.

Run stripes in this direction.

Medallion Star
M2

Treasure Boxes

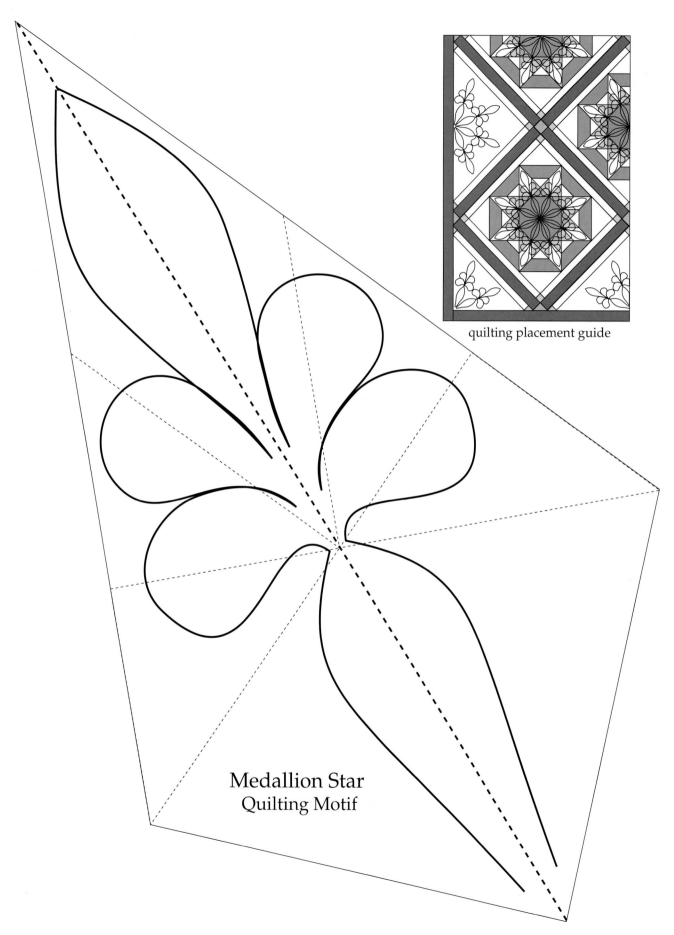

quilting placement guide

Medallion Star
Quilting Motif

LESSON PLANS
for
Stack-n-Whackier Quilts

Teachers and shop owners are welcome to develop classes using this book as a textbook. Please remember that the book's copyright prohibits photocopying or other printing of any materials herein, with the exception of the Guides and Patterns on pages 122–131, which may be copied for personal use only. Here are some suggestions for lesson plans to fit various class schedules.

Three-Hour Class

Students bring the main fabric only. They can make one stack, cut block kits from one strip, and begin piecing the blocks. The teacher should demonstrate the remaining steps for finishing the blocks and discuss the setting and finishing steps.

Recommended Projects: SECRET STAIRWAYS, FAN QUILT.

Five to Six-Hour Class

Students bring the main fabric and any additional fabrics needed to piece the blocks. They can make one stack, cut block kits, and piece several blocks. For intermediate-level classes, students can cut some of the background or accent fabrics before class.

Recommended Projects: SECRET STAIRWAYS, TREASURE BOXES, SARA'S ROSES, FAN QUILT. KAREN'S TRANSPARENT STAR, ROUNDABOUT STARS, NOVELTY WINDOWS, and ARGYLE DIAMONDS are suitable, if students have assistance in selecting appropriate fabrics before the class.

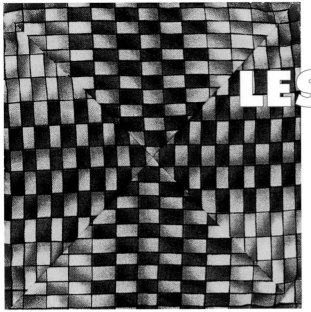

LESSON PLANS
for
Stack-n-Whackier Quilts
(continued)

Two Three-Hour Classes

This format has the advantage of allowing students to cut the main fabric block kits before selecting the companion fabrics.

SESSION 1: Students cut the block kits, learning the Stack-n-Whack method, and begin piecing the blocks. Allow time at the end of class to preview background and accent fabrics.

SESSION 2: Students finish piecing some or all the blocks and learn any additional techniques used for the project, such as appliqué. Review setting and finishing steps.

Recommended Projects: SECRET STAIRWAYS and the FAN QUILT are good choices for mixed skill levels. KAREN'S TRANSPARENT STAR, NOVELTY WINDOWS, and ARGYLE DIAMONDS are also suitable, if students have assistance in selecting appropriate fabrics before the first class. The BUTTERFLIES and MEADOW FLOWERS projects are appropriate for intermediate-level classes.

Four Two-Hour Classes

This longer format allows more time to help with fabric selection and layout decisions, so it is especially beneficial for beginners. Intermediate and advanced students can try the more challenging projects.

SESSION 1: Cut the main fabric for the blocks and preview the block kits on various backgrounds. Students can then cut the background fabric at home.

SESSION 2: Begin sewing the blocks. Often, students can complete the blocks at home before the third session.

SESSION 3: Complete the blocks and choose an arrangement. Pin the blocks to a sheet to keep them in order. Begin preparing the setting or border pieces.

SESSION 4: Set the quilt together. Discuss quilting and finishing options.

Recommended Projects: NOVELTY WINDOWS, ARGYLE DIAMONDS, and any of the projects in Part Two are suitable for beginners in this format. For intermediate quilters, consider MEDALLION STAR, VENETIAN TILES, and the Magic Mirror-Image projects as well.

BIBLIOGRAPHY

Magic Stack-n-Whack techniques and designs

Reynolds, Bethany. *Magic Stack-n-Whack™ Quilts*. American Quilter's Society, Paducah, KY, 1998.

Reynolds, Bethany. *Stars a la Carte*. American Quilter's Society, Paducah, KY, 2000.

Selecting fabrics for dimensional effects

Combs, Karen. *Optical Illusions for Quilters*. American Quilter's Society, Paducah, KY, 1997.

Machine-quilting techniques

Noble, Maurine. *Machine Quilting Made Easy*. That Patchwork Place, Bothell, WA, 1994.

Noble, Maurine and Elizabeth Hendricks. *Machine Quilting with Decorative Threads*. That Patchwork Place, Bothell, WA, 1994.

Machine appliqué and embellishing techniques

Roberts, Sharee Dawn. *Creative Machine Arts*. American Quilter's Society, Paducah, KY, 1992.

SOURCES

BSR Design, Inc.
P.O. Box 1374
Ellsworth, ME 04605
website: http://www.quilt.com/BReynolds
Patterns, workshops, and lectures by Bethany Reynolds

Clearview Triangle
8311-180th St. S.E.
Snohomish, WA 98296-4802
888-901-4151
Super 60™ and other triangles for cutting 60° designs; books and patterns by Sara Nephew, with many designs adaptable for Stack-n-Whack™

J.D. Services
2147 Broadway
Grand Junction, CO 81503
800-835-7817
Custom acrylic templates for any shape

J.T. Trading Corporation
P.O. Box 9439
Bridgeport, CT 06601-9439
203-339-4904
Basting spray for appliqué and quilting

Karen Combs
1405 Creekview Court
Columbia, TN 38401
931-490-0618 (fax)
website: www.karencombs.com
Custom templates, patterns, workshops, and lectures

Phillips Fiber Art
PO Box 173
Fruita, CO 81521
800-982-8166
Wedge templates and books by Cheryl Phillips, with many designs adaptable for Stack-n-Whack™

PineTree Quiltworks
585 Broadway
South Portland, ME 04106
207-799-7357
website: http//www.quiltworks.com
Quilting fabrics and supplies, including the acrylic Stack-n-Whack 45° Triangle Tool and Fan Rulers; patterns by Bethany Reynolds

Other AQS Books

This is only a small selection of the books available from the American Quilter's Society. AQS books are known worldwide for timely topics, clear writing, beautiful color photos, and accurate illustrations and patterns. The following books are available from your local bookseller, quilt shop, or public library.

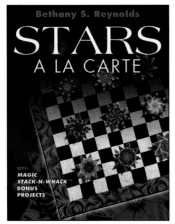

#5589   US$21.95

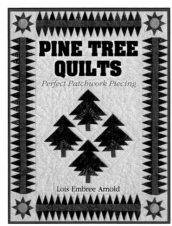

#5708   US$22.95

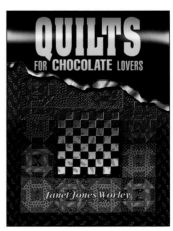

#5758   US$19.95

#5755   US$21.95

#4995   US$19.95

#5756   US$19.95

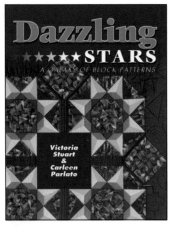

#5844   US$21.95

#5764   US$19.95

#5848   US$19.95

Look for these books nationally or call **1-800-626-5420**